Divine Craftsmanship

Preliminaries to a Spirituality of Work

JEAN HANI

Divine Craftsmanship

*Preliminaries to
a Spirituality of Work*

⊕

ANGELICO PRESS
SOPHIA PERENNIS

Originally published in French as
Les Métiers de Dieu
© Guy Trédaniel, Éditions de la Maisnie, 1975
First published in USA
by Sophia Perennis © 2007
Angelico Press/Sophia Perennis edition © 2016

Translated by Robert Proctor
Edited by G. John Champoux and Marie Hansen
Series editor: James R. Wetmore

For information, address:
Angelico Press
4709 Briar Knoll Dr.
Kettering, OH 45429
angelicopress.com

Library of Congress Cataloging-in-Publication Data

Hani, Jean.
[Métiers de Dieu. English]
Divine craftsmanship: preliminaries to a
spirituality of work /Jean Hani.

p. cm.
ISBN 1 59731 068 0 (pbk: alk. paper)
1. Spiritual life—Christianity. I. Title.
BV4502.H3613 2006
261.5'6—dc22   s2006021560

Cover Design: Michael Schrauzer

CONTENTS

Introduction

THE FOLLOWING PAGES were originally intended as part of a more important work on the relations between active and contemplative life. This question merits particular attention today when so much is said, and so badly, about restoring the dignity of work. But such a restoration will only be possible to the extent that we rediscover the true principles upon which this dignity is based.

The following reflections aim to recall these principles in part, which is also why they fall within the framework of the general topic just mentioned. However, these reflections not only evolved into something unanticipated, but developed along definite lines that gave them a particular unity and certain emphases, so much so that we thought it preferable to write a separate book. This, while serving as an introduction to the other work, will allow us to approach the question of the spirituality of the active life from a more specific angle, and thereby already glimpse some of its repercussions in the life of a society. One will find a short but excellent introduction to the spirituality of the active life in Marco Pallis' book, *The Way and the Mountain*.[1]

These preliminary remarks are necessary in order to define the object and method of the present study. We do not want to expound all of the metaphysical foundations of a spirituality of the active life—of functions and occupations—nor the modalities of their application in the practical domain. Our intention here is only to lay the initial foundations of this spirituality, that is to say, to show that all functions and occupations can and should be seen as reflections of Divine Activity, and if reflections, therefore also

---

1. Peter Owen edition, London, 1961.

1

symbols of this Activity. Our study is above all intended to be a descriptive analysis of these symbols, for only symbols let us grasp in a concrete and, so to say, vital way, the doctrinal foundation we are discussing.

But why the title 'Divine Craftsmanship' with its suggestion that God is some kind of skilled workman? Is not this manner of expression somewhat paradoxical or even irreverent? Let us hasten to say that the choice of these words was not made from any desire to be novel or provocative; to our mind, they conform completely to the nature of things. If human occupations with their associated craftsmanship are symbols of Divine Activity, one can with perfect legitimacy speak of Divine craftsmanship and the occupations of God. This is because human occupations in fact exist in God in an 'eminent' fashion; or, if one prefers, in God there exist the archetypes of the different human activities. What is more, the Scriptures themselves speak of the occupations of God, who appears in them at different times with the traits of a shepherd, a reaper, or vine-grower, etc. And this is natural. The moment divine anthropomorphism is admitted, every aspect of the human condition can in some way be assumed by God. Now anthropomorphism should certainly be admitted, since it comes to us from Scripture, that is to say, from God himself.

But it will also be said that to speak of God's occupations and skills can only be a literary metaphor: by its means an operation of the mind is transposed, something that in reality belongs only to the human order is projected into the Divine Order. The formulation perhaps has poetical but not ontological value. Nothing could be further from the mark. If it were only a question of literature or poetry, we would not have gone to the trouble of undertaking this work, the foundations of which, in that case, would have been very fragile. Undoubtedly, there *is* a transposition from the human to the divine order in the manifestations of symbolic thought we are about to describe, but only in the order of *knowing*, not of *being*. The mind crosses from the human to the divine occupation as it crosses from the *sensible* to the *intelligible*, which is not to say that the intelligible is not preexistent in the sensible. In the same way, we shall discover that our activities, in their order, are a reflection of

Divine Activity, in Its Order, and realize that our activities exist in the Divine Order, but in a different mode, which is properly the *principial*, or, if preferred, the *archetypal*, if this latter term be understood in its traditional and Platonic sense, that is to say, as designating a thing existing in God as *idea*, and not after the manner of modern psychologists, who reduce archetypes to expressions of a purely psychological and human, nay collective and infra-human, order.

To use an ancient image, this existence in principial mode can be compared to radii that are already integrally present in the center of the circle.

> Just as there is this unique point at the center of the circle where all the straight lines extending from it are still undivided, so, in God, he who has been judged worthy to arrive at this point knows all the ideas of created beings with a knowledge that is both simple and without concepts.[2]

In the last resort, the reference to the divine archetype is, moreover, founded upon the following statement of Christ: 'My Father has never ceased working, and I too must be at work' (John 5:17). This continuous divine activity is Creation. It is symbolized in Genesis as an event that took place in primordial times, but in reality is a continuous activity. As Meister Eckhart said in one of his sermons, 'God did not create the world 6000 years ago, but creates it in this very moment', in this 'indivisible now' (*atomon nyn*), to use Aristotle's expression. God, however, wished to share this continuous activity with His creatures; to the heavenly, angelic Powers, He apportioned the stars that revolve in cosmic space, and to man, the earth, represented in the Biblical account as a garden. 'And the Lord God took the man, and put him into the garden of Eden to dress it and to keep it' (Gen. 2:15). Agricultural work, the foremost occupation, since it is indispensable to human life, is here taken for work as such: it is emblematic of work in itself and, more generally, of Action in all its forms. To practice a trade is to act upon the world with a view to transforming it; it is, consequently, to extend God's

---

2. Maximus the Confessor, *Chapters on Knowledge*, 2, 4.

work. The latter is the model and synthesis of all occupations. In reality, God is the only Artisan: according to the Scholastic adage *Unus artifex est Deus.*[3] All occupations imitate God, Who is ceaselessly at work, for He ceaselessly creates the world. And this, in the final analysis, is the sole basis of their dignity.

3. Cited by J. Maritain, *Frontières de la Poésie*, p9. Cf. the expression 'Maker of the Universe' applied to God by St Clement of Rome, *Epistle to the Corinthians*, in *Apostolic Fathers* (Lightfoot trans.). An exactly corresponding form of this Divine epithet is found in Ancient Egypt: *hemou-ta* (S. Morenz, *La Relig. egypt.*, 1962, p213).

1

The
Divine Scribe

A STUDY OF 'Divine Craftsmanship' should normally begin with
the two highest occupations or skills of God: the priesthood and
kingship, except that these are no longer occupations properly so-
called, but rather functions. These two functions are those of
teacher and sacrificer, governor and judge, spiritual authority and
temporal power, and are the immediate and most elevated reflections of the divine activity *ad extra*, and in particular of the Divine
Word. As these functions go beyond the very notion of occupation,
we shall postpone speaking of them until we come to explain the
foundations of a sacred politics and sociology. We shall therefore
concentrate *in divinis* on three occupations attached to and, to an
extent, specifications of these two functions: the scribe, the physician and the warrior.

In principle, all languages are sacred because their constituent element, speech, or the word, is but an attenuated form of Primordial
Speech, the Divine Word, which is the direct source of the creative
act, as is shown by the following two quotations from Scripture:
'God *said*: Let there be light!' (Gen. 1:3); and, 'In the beginning was
the Word...' (John 1:1). As it is written, because of language's fundamental sanctity we shall have to account for 'every idle word'; to
utter an idle word is, in fact, somewhat equivalent to 'taking the
Name of God [as essential Word] in vain'. The sacredness of speech
naturally extends to writing, which is the fixation of Sound—*aerial*
by nature—and as if its crystallization in an *earthly* element. The
letters used in writing always derive originally from hieroglyphs,

5

that is to say from sacred symbolic characters, the receptacles of the different 'words' designating the essence of things. This is why the handling of letters, or the art of writing, like the function of teaching, constitutes a skill directly related to the sacred, especially as literature itself is always originally sacred. The scribe, like the cleric, therefore belongs by right to the priestly order, which directly represents the divine order on earth. The ancient Egyptians expressed this when they made scribes dependants of the god Thoth, known as the 'Scribe of Maat', that is to say, of Divine Truth and Justice. And so it is not surprising to see God, as the Word, shown as having the traits and functions of a scribe.

We are familiar with the images of Christ in glory adorning the tympana of church entrances: the Lord sitting on a throne, blessing with his right hand, while in his left he holds an open book. This is the evocation of Christ as the Judge at the end of time; the book is the Book of Life, *liber vitae*, in which both the actions of men and the names of the elect are recorded.[1] Elsewhere, in ordinary icons of the Savior based on the same model, the book is the Scriptures, for in this instance the Lord sits as a teacher.

However, in these various representations, the book also has a far wider meaning, of which those just mentioned are only particular applications. In all cases we are dealing with the Book of the World, *liber mundi*, that is to say, of the whole of creation, of which God is then considered to be the Scribe. This is indicated in particular by the two letters A and Ω which are generally carved upon it.[2]

Here we encounter a typically Semitic symbolism, which is better understood in the light of the Judaic and Islamic traditions, where it is far more developed than in Christianity. In these traditions the Book is held to be the supreme mode of Revelation, where it plays the role taken by Christ himself for Christians; indeed, it can be said

---

1. *Apoc.* 3:5, *Phil.* 4:3, *Exod.* 32:32, *Psalm* 68:138. In its most external form, this scene takes its inspiration from royal assizes during the course of which the prince opened the household account-book containing the names of his people in order to render accounts.

2. Although ancient, this idea of the *Liber Mundi* is particularly developed in Rosicrucian literature. References in Sédir, *Hist. d. Rose-Croix*, pp124–25.

that in these religions the Word is made Book, whereas for Christians He is made Flesh. But the symbolism of the Book and Scribe nevertheless exists in Christianity, although in not so clear a form. We can thus quite legitimately draw inspiration from Judaism and Islam in order to throw light upon the applications of this symbolism in Christian thought and iconography, for the latter has absorbed the most elements of this tradition and by means of it we will be better able to explain the texts and certain rites.

According, then, to the Semitic traditions, God created the world after the manner of a book.

The universe is this book, and its letters are the elements; the elements in turn, through their indefinite combinations under the influence of Divine Thought, produce creatures and things. Thus, words and phrases appear as manifestations of creative possibilities. This book is obviously inseparable from the Divine Word, just as, with a human author, the book is nothing but a materialization of the inner word. We can say that in a way the Divine Word is 'crystallized' in the Book of the World.[3]

The Muslim mystic Ibn al-'Arabi, basing himself on the *hadiths*,[4] expounded this symbolism very well when he said that

> the Universe is a vast *book*; the *characters* of this book are all written, in principle, with the same *ink* and transcribed on to the eternal *Tablet* by the Divine *Pen*; all are transcribed simultaneously and inseparably; for that reason the essential phenomena hidden in the 'secret of secrets' were given the name of 'transcendent letters'. And these same transcendent letters, that is to say all creatures, after having been virtually condensed in the

---

3. F. Schuon, *Understanding Islam*, tr. D.M. Matheson (Baltimore: Penguin Books, 1972), pp51–52. Schuon quite rightly adds that this can be considered on three levels: In God himself the Word is Being as Eternal Act, the Book is Being as the sum total of creation's possibilities (Wisdom); on a lower level, the Word is the Creating Act, the Book the creative substance, *materia prima*; finally, in creation itself, the Word is the Divine Spirit, the Book the sum total of creation.

4. The *hadith* are the sayings of Muhammad, forming one of the major pillars of Islam.

Divine Omniscience, were carried down on the Divine Breath to the lower lines, and composed and formed the manifested Universe.[5]

The *hadiths* specify that the Ink flows and the divine Pen writes until the Day of Resurrection.

The symbolism of letters and the Book is even more developed in the Hebraic tradition, where the Torah, that is, the Bible, the Book of the Scriptures, is identified with the supreme Wisdom which issues from God to give existence to the universe. The Rabbinical tradition, above all in its mystical dimension, develops this symbolism on the basis of passages from the Torah such as the following: 'Thy eyes beheld my unformed substance; in thy book were written, every one of them, the days that were formed for me, when as yet there was none of them' (Psalm 138:16). These verses envisage the symbolism of the book at the level of individual human destiny, but it is easy to see that its transposition to Creation in general is legitimate and even necessary.

This transposition is concretized in a mystical book, the *Sepher Yetsira* or 'book of the creation', which is presented as a commentary on Genesis.[6] According to the *Sepher Yetsira*, God created the universe as a book through the combination of numbers and letters. In other words the Divine Word or Speech produced the world and man through the creative power of the letters composing the Word and the numbers ordering these letters.

The essential numbers are 10, 3, 7, and 12, the last three being those into which the 22 letters of the Hebrew alphabet can be divided. The

---

5. From *Al-Futuhat al-Mekkiyah* cited by R. Guénon, *The Symbolism of the Cross* (Ghent, NY: Sophia Perennis, 2001), p78. We can find the texts of the *hadiths* and the explanation of the metaphysical sense of the various symbols, such as tablet, ink, pen, etc., in F. Schuon, *Dimensions of Islam* (tr. P. N. Townsend, London: Allen and Unwin, 1969), pp102–108. An analogous general formulation is found in an Eastern Christian text, where we read that God gave to the angels the following explanation of the creation He was about to make: 'As with a Pen, He wrote them a book in the spirit and caused them to meditate on the writings of universal creation.' (Nasrai, *Homily* 34 (On the Divine Essence), in *OS*, 8 (1963), 247).

6. On the *Sepher Yetsira*, see H. Serouya, *La Kabbale*, pp128–38; P. Vulliaud, *La Kabbale juive*, II, pp214–15.

number 10 corresponds to the *sephiroth* or creative energies, and the numbers $3+7+12=22$ to the energies of the alphabet; their total, 32, constitutes the '32 Ways of Wisdom', that is to say, the ways in which Wisdom realizes the universe.

The letters were engraved in the primordial Air that issued from the Divine Breath. They are, first, the three mother letters: A, M, and Sh, corresponding to the three primordial elements: Air, Water, and Fire, the three principal seasons (in the East), and the three major parts of the human body: the head, heart, and abdomen. Then there are the seven letters of dual aspiration, b, bh, k, kh, etc., that represent the principle of duality inherent in created being: life-death, male-female, etc.... the planets, the days of the week, and the seven openings of the body. And, finally, the twelve other letters, corresponding to the Zodiac, the twelve months, and twelve senses and faculties of man.[7]

Thus the cosmos has 22 parts which one finds reflected in the human microcosm. These 22 parts or elements constitute the 22 'letters' of the cosmic Alphabet.[8]

Many rabbis have given commentaries on the *Sepher Yetsira*, especially Ibn-Gabirol, who thoroughly explained the principle of its symbolism. He wrote,

> The (divine) Will, which acts (in order to impress form on matter), that is to say, to carry out (creation), can be compared to an Author; form, the product of action, is like Scripture, and matter, which serves them as substratum, is like the Tablet or Paper.[9]

---

7. Sight, hearing, smell, touch, speech, nutrition, generation, locomotion, anger, joy, thought, and sleep.

8. Man, as the foundation of the world, is the alphabet of the world, and this corresponds to the fact that, in Genesis, God brought the living things to him 'that he might name them.' Man is the alphabet, in reflection, from which all beings are assembled. (Ph. D'Aquin, *Interprétation de l'Arbre de la Kabbale*, pp 28–30). Note also that the alphabet issues from the *sephiroth*: the letters from Binah, the points from Hokmah, the accents from Kether (P. Vulliaud, loc. cit.).

9. Ibn-Gabirol, *La Source de Vie*, ed. Munk, in *Mel. De philos. juive et arabe*, pp 135–6. On the ternary *sepher, saphar, sippur* (book, scribe, word, or matter, will, form), see Mayer Lambert cited in H. Serouya, op. cit. p 130 and Vulliaud, op. cit.

This passage provides a good summary of the Semitic symbolism of the Divine Book and Scribe.

As stated at the outset, the preceding remarks will enable us to highlight certain aspects of Christian iconography and ritual, and, ultimately, to come to a particularly enriched 'reading' of the Bible.

Let us first revisit the icon of the Savior in Glory holding the Book. It is a plastic figuration of the theophany of the Apocalypse, which is suggested, notably, by the frequent presence on the book of the letters A and Ω, by which Christ designated Himself: 'I am the Alpha and the Omega, the First and the Last' (Apoc. 22:13), 'I am the Alpha and the Omega, the Beginning and the End' (ibid. 1:8 and 21:6).[10] The Lord is the First because it is He who creates; He is the Beginning, the Principle of all things, the absolute efficient Cause; and He is also the Last, for it is He who, in the widest sense of the word, judges, that is, who leads all things to their end; and He is Himself this End, the absolute Final Cause.[11] This first ontological truth in the order of relationships between the created and the Creator is expressed in the symbolism of the two extreme letters of the Greek alphabet, A and Ω;[12] these two letters are like the synthesis, the summary of the whole alphabet, implicitly containing all the intermediate letters. In the light of what was said above, it will be readily understood that these letters included between the two extremes symbolize all creatures, which are so many particular forms

<hr>

10. The formula is already in the Old Testament: 'I am the First and the Last' (Isaiah 41:4, 44:6, 48:12), which explains its reappearance in Islam: 'He is the First and the Last (*al-awwal wa-l-akhir*)' (Quran 57:3). See on this subject F. Schuon, 'Dimensions of the Universe in the Quranic doctrine of the Divine Names' in *Dimensions of Islam*, pp30–45. It belongs equally to Orphism under a similar form: 'God is the Beginning, God is the Middle, God is the Origin of all things' (*Orph. Frag.* VI, 10. Cf. Plutarch, *De def. orac.*, 48).

11. On the properly metaphysical plane A and Ω, the First and the Last, signify that God is Himself His own origin and end.

12. Here the Greek alphabet is naturally a substitute for the Hebrew alphabet, the two extreme letters of which are A and Th.

uttered by the Word, forms crystallized as it were in letters and inscribed in the *Liber mundi* or the *Liber vitae.*[13]

From this representation of Christ in Glory, we move to another, also inspired by the Apocalypse, that of the Lamb lying on the Book with Seven Seals (5:1–8), at the summit of the mountain whence flow the four rivers of living water. What is involved here is the mountain of paradise with its four rivers, the common source of which is situated at the center of the world, but also, more generally, an image of the world.[14] This situation clearly indicates that the Book with Seven Seals is, again, the *Liber mundi*; the seals, which are only to be broken by the Lamb, are related to the seven ages of the world according to Judaeo-Christian tradition.[15]

The mysticism of letters also explains certain details in the rituals for the consecration of churches and the blessing of water.

The inscription of the double alphabet, Greek and Latin (and formerly also Hebrew), in the large cross of ashes traced on the floor of a new church, can only be satisfactorily explained from this point of view. There are undoubtedly vestiges of the Jewish letter-mysticism in this practice. It has been well said by Paul Vulliaud that the Church, in tracing the letters of the alphabet in the temple, lays out there the elements of its teaching, just as God laid out the elements in the temple of the world in order to reveal His Perfections.[16] And

---

13. The Jewish tradition considers creation as a revelation of the Name of God through letters and numbers. In particular, it is known that the Four Animals of the Apocalypse placed at the four corners of Christ in Glory are related to the four letters of the Name YHWH. The image of the book representing the whole of creation is even in Dante. In the final vision of Paradise, he perceived all creatures gathered together in the Divine Light:

> *Nel suo profondo vidi che s'interna*
> *Legato con amore in un volume*
> *Cio che per l'universo si squaderna.* (*Par.* 33,85).

> [*In its depths, bound in a book by love,*
> *I saw assembled all the beings*
> *that in the world are scattered leaves.*]

14. See our book *The Symbolism of the Christian Temple*, p107.

15. This obviously does not prevent the attribution to them of other perfectly legitimate meanings.

16. Op. cit., I, p214.

further, since the temple is a summary of the world and an image of the Body of Christ, the letters traced on the paving then represent not only the elements of the teaching, but indeed the totality of creatures and things in the world, all contained in the divine Word, like the letters between A and Ω.[17]

We believe the insufflation in the form of *psi* at the moment of the solemn blessing of the waters at Easter can rightly be connected to the same symbolic context. The ritual expressly relates this gesture to the prologue of Genesis, which evokes the Spirit of God moving over the waters. The Greek letter *psi*, having this form: ψ, is the first letter of the word *psyche*, which, in fact, means breath or soul. Interpreted in this way, the rite already becomes quite eloquent. But perhaps its true significance is even more profound. It is, in fact, rather curious that a rite effecting the descent of the Holy Spirit should use the word *psyche*, which denotes the breath of life or individual soul, and is not used in Scripture to denote the divine Spirit, which is rendered by *pneuma*. Everything leads us to believe that the Greek letter *psi* is, in this instance, a substitute for the Hebraic letter *shin*, ש, which, except for the lower branch, has an analogous form and is traditionally taken as the hieroglyph of the Divine Fire and symbol of the Word: ψ.[18]

Thus the rite of sanctification of the baptismal waters represents the descent of the Spirit into the water after the manner of a sacred letter imprinted upon a material; water is, moreover, a well-known symbol of *Materia prima*.

In closing, we shall again make a comment inspired by the symbolism of letters and writing, but of a much more general order, since it concerns the Bible as a whole.

We said above that, for the Israelites, the Torah is identical to Supreme Wisdom issuing from God in order to give existence to the universe, a conception considerably illuminated by an explanation

---

17. These considerations are more broadly developed in our book, *The Symbolism of the Christian Temple*, pp 34–40.

18. Concerning the fact that, very often in the New Testament, Greek grammatical forms, the choice of which seems strange at first, hide Hebraic forms, see P. Vulliaud, *La Clé traditionnelle des Évangiles* (passim).

of letter symbolism. What riches can we not extract from this teaching in support of a particular 'reading' of the Bible! Within this perspective, the Bible is truly the Book of the World and the Book of Life. Opening with Genesis and closing with the Apocalypse, it includes everything essential concerning the world and man: the history of the world, whence it comes, whither it goes, what it is; the story of man, the secret of his destiny, of his beginning and end; the relations between man and the world, and the laws governing them; finally the principles of morality, mysticism, and all the sciences.[19] We are now in a position to see the Bible not as *a* book, but as *the* Book, the book of all the secrets of creation, the Living Book that the divine Scribe, who has 'the words of eternal life', never ceases writing.

19. Here we are obviously speaking of the traditional sciences, the only true ones, modern sciences, proud of having become profane, as if this were a matter of progress, being rightly but parodies of the veritable sciences.

2

Christ
the Physician

IF THE PRIEST is *scribe*, he is also *physician*. The first function reflects the Logos as creator, the second, as preserver and savior. That is why in His earthly incarnation, Christ, who was Savior, was also physician. And the importance of this role of Jesus cannot be exaggerated. The Gospel is full of accounts of His miraculous healings: healings of the blind (Matt. 9:27–31, 12:22, 20:30–34), of Peter's mother-in-law (Mark 1:29–34), of the centurion's servant (Matt. 8:5-13), of the woman with an issue of blood (ibid., 9:20–22), of the man with dropsy (Luke 14:2–8), of the lepers (Matt. 8:2–4), of the paralytic (John 5), of the mad child (Matt. 17:14-20), of the withered hand (ibid., 12:10–13), of the son of the nobleman from Capernaum (John 4:46-54), of the deaf mute (Mark 9:32–37), of the demoniacs and possessed (Matt. 8:28–34, 15:21–28, 12:22–23, 9:32–34). During the meal with Levi, Jesus alluded to his role as physician: 'They that are whole have no need of the physician, but they that are sick. I came not to call the righteous, but sinners to repentance' (Mark 2:17, Luke 5:32). And His first sermon at Nazareth began in that way: 'Doubtless, you will apply to me the proverb: Physician heal thyself' (Luke 4:23).

Furthermore, Isaiah had already predicted concerning the Messiah: 'Surely he hath borne our griefs, and carried our sorrows' (53:4). And St Peter echoed him by revering in Jesus 'Him through whose wounds men have been healed' (1 Pet. 2:24).

The conception of Christianity as a religion of healing and salvation, the two ideas being intimately linked, immediately found an echo in the Greco-Roman world,[1] where there was an established connection between physician (*iatros*), savior (*soter*), and philosopher. The latter was at that time something quite different from what is today called a philosopher. During an age when faith in the old polytheism was foundering, philosophy had replaced religion, at the very least among the elite, and, in the world, the philosopher to some extent played the role of a director of conscience. He really did heal, soothing pains, helping people to bear physical maladies, and treating and healing moral evil. It is thus that Epicurus was often represented as a physician, and his four moral precepts stated the ideal dressing for all of humanity's woes.[2] Parallel to this there was the very popular ancient cult of Asklepios, the god of healing, who, moreover, became a 'universal savior'[3] during the Imperial epoch and, in Alexandrian hermeticism, an intercessor between man and the divinity.[4]

To better ensure the triumph of the new faith, the Greek apologists, nourished by both the Bible and Hellenism, strove to present the Messiah as the perfect Philosopher, at once savior and physician. St Justin exalted the Christ who healed the maimed, the deaf, the lame, the blind, and the dead.[5] For Clement of Alexandria, the Word was 'the universal redresser of human weaknesses, the charmer of wounded souls.'[6] According to Eusebius, a prince of Osroene was won over to Christ at the end of the second century through his admiration for 'his cures without herbs, without medicaments.'[7] The Latin apologists St Cyprian and Tertullian developed

---

1. On this subject, see Harnack, *Die Mission und Ausbreitung des Christentumsin den ersten drei Jahrhunderten*, pp87 ff. and J. Carcopino, *Aspects mystiques de la Rome païenne*, pp244–7.

2. J. Carcopino, loc. cit.

3. Ael. Arist., *In Asclep.* 42,4 (p336 Keil).

4. References in Carcopino, op. cit., pp258–59. Cf. further Plutarch, *De sera* 4 (cf. 19–21): 'God knows the best time to apply chastisements for crimes, just as the enlightened physician knows how to administer remedies, varying the dose and the time depending on the circumstances.'

5. *Dialogue with Trypho*, 69.

6. Clement of Alexandria, *Instructor*, 1, 2, 6.

7. Eusebius, *Ecclesiastical History*, 1, 13. Cf. St Ignatius of Antioch, for whom Christ was a 'physician of flesh and spirit' (*To the Ephesians.* 7, 2; Lightfoot, p65).

the same theme,[8] while St Augustine called Jesus *medicus magnus, onmipotens medicus, medicus et salvator mundi*.[9]

Archeology confirms the spread of the motif of Christ the physician. An acclamation discovered in a chapel at Timgad was worded as follows: '*Subveni, Christe, tu solus medicus*' (Come down, O Christ, thou the sole physician),[10] and the miraculous cures of Our Lord were constantly represented in the paintings of the Catacombs and on fourth- and fifth-century sarcophagi.

Right from the start, the theme has always inspired the liturgy. The notion of *Christus medicus* is encountered in a prayer dating from at least the second century, where we read: 'Efface our blemishes through Our Lord Jesus Christ, Thine Only Son, the all-holy and physician of our souls.'[11] And it has continued to nourish the poetry of hymns: 'So that the universe might not succumb to the ruses of the devil, Thou didst, in a surge of love, make Thyself the physician of the world.'[12] 'Physician of our souls, heal me, wounded by the blade of sin, shattered by my many crimes: apply the remedy of Thy wise commandments, O Clement One!'[13] In this instance, Christ's medicine is His commandments; elsewhere it is fasting; above all it is the Sacraments that constitute the medicine of eternal life.[14] Clement of Alexandria refers to baptism as 'the infallible remedy',[15] but before all else, the Eucharist is the medicine of immortality, the *pharmakon athanasias*. The motif of the Eucharist as remedy is as developed as that of the Eucharist as nourishment. In the Mass, it inspires the prayers that precede and follow Communion: 'that the taking of Thy Body, Lord Jesus Christ, will not be unto me for judgment nor condemnation, but for sustenance and unto *healing of soul and body...*' After that, the *Domine non sum dignus* (Lord, I am not worthy): 'Say but a word, and my *soul shall be healed*.' Then

---

8. Tertullian, *Adv. Marc.* III, 17; St Cyprian, *De op.*, 1.
9. St Augustine, *Serm.* 175, 1; 299, 6; 87, 11; *Enarr. in Psalm.* 130, 7.
10. RA, 1920, pp17–18; CRAI, 1920, p77; RCAP, 1923.
11. Berlin Papyrus (second cent.) in PO 18,430.
12. Advent Hymn *Creator alme siderum*.
13. Triodion, second week Lent, AL, Lent, p197.
14. Prayer of Tuesday of Holy Week and of Saturday after Ash Wednesday.
15. Clem. of Alex., *Instructor.* I, 6, 29.

the prayer recited during the final ablutions: 'That the gift given in this life may be unto us a *remedy for life eternal.*' Finally, the prayer after communion often resumes the theme while paraphrasing it: 'Grant, Lord, that this sacrament which we have received may be profitable to us for the *healing of soul and body...*'(Trinity Sunday). 'Enable us, Lord, to feel in our soul and our body, the sustaining power of Thy Sacrament ... *the heavenly remedy*' (Second Sunday after Pentecost).[16]

The importance afforded this theme of Christ the physician by Scripture and Tradition merits pause and reflection. All the texts we have cited emphasize the parallel and close union between the healing of soul and body. On many occasions, Christ affirmed that physical evil is linked to moral evil, that the true cause of sickness, as of sin, is the work of demons, and, finally, that it is faith that both heals and saves. He tells the paralytic at the Pool of Bethsaida: 'Behold, thou art made whole: sin no more, lest a worse thing come unto thee' (John 5:14).

Health, like salvation, can only come from Jesus. As the Divine Word, Christ is Life, for it is written: 'I am the Way, the Truth and the Life,' and 'In Him was the Life,' and again 'In Thee is the source of life.' The Word is Universal Life, the master not only of physical, but also of psychic and spiritual life. The Gospel says that 'from Him there came forth a power that healed' (Luke 6:19); this power was the manifestation on the physical plane of the Energy that is Universal Life in the Divine Word. Physical life and the health of the body are dependent upon spiritual life and energy, and here we have a truth all but forgotten in our modern world which has artificially separated the soul from the body, health from salvation.

---

16. One could cite many post-communion prayers, for example those of the first Sunday after Easter, the seventeenth and twenty-fourth after Pentecost, the Friday of the fourth week of Lent, and Thursday of Holy Week. — The *pharmakon athanasias* has sometimes been assimilated to the plant *moly* (*Odyssey*, 10, 302–6) in the Christian psychotherapy of the Greek tradition. On this subject see H. Rahner, *Greek Myths and Christian Mysteries*, tr. B. Battershaw (New York and Evanston: Harper and Row, 1963), pp181–222. — These communion prayers are ancient: one finds them in an analogous form in the *Sacramentary of Serapion* (fourth cent.), Eng. tr. J. Wordsworth, *Bishop Serapion's Prayer Book* (Hamden, CT: Archon Books, 1964).

This dependence of health upon spiritual life explains why medicine was traditionally never a profane science, as it has become today, but a sacred science that formed part of the Priestly Art, and was the prerogative of priests or their assistants.[17] In fact, only He who is the Master of Life can, on His own or through His representatives, act totally upon life.

The connection between medical and priestly skills is admirably demonstrated in the fact that one traditional image is at the same time the emblem of medicine and one of the symbols of Christ the Savior: we refer to the staff of Aesculapius, sometimes incorrectly called the caduceus, a vertical staff with a serpent coiled around it,[18] which is identical to the *brazen serpent*, one of the major symbols of Christ.

We recall that in the story of the brazen serpent, the Hebrews were bitten by fiery serpents during their long wanderings in the desert. Moses asked God what he should do, and God commanded him to fashion a serpent from brass and place it before the people. 'And Moses made a serpent of brass, and put it upon a pole, and it came to pass, that if a serpent had bitten any man, when he beheld the serpent of brass, he lived' (Num. 21:6-9). The brazen serpent was subsequently placed in the temple and remained there until the time of King Hezekiah (Kings 2:18).

It was already known in the Old Testament that this serpent was in fact a 'sign', the sign of the Messiah, seeing that we read in the *Book of Wisdom*: 'He who looked at the serpent was not healed by the object he saw, but by Thee, Savior of men' (16:7). And Christ Himself made a point of confirming this testimony: 'As Moses lifted up the serpent in the wilderness, even so must the Son of man be

---

17. To be exact, it is necessary to distinguish between the miraculous thaumaturgic medicine of Christ and the saints, and the Art of Medicine, which is a theoretical and practical science, but nevertheless, in traditional societies, always based upon metaphysical principles of which the priesthood is custodian.

18. In the case of the caduceus, the emblem of Hermes, there are two coiled serpents, facing each other at eye level; under consideration here is the fundamental polarization of energy into two currents, active and passive, positive and negative (*yang-yin*).

lifted up: that whosoever believeth in him should not perish, but have eternal life' (John 3:14–15).[19]

This typology was widely exploited in subsequent Christian ages, both by the Fathers and in sacred hymns and holy images. Its lines of development are clearly outlined by Tertullian, for example, who asked:

> Why did Moses . . . set up the golden serpent on the pole; and as it hung there, propose it as an object to be looked at for a cure? Did he not here also intend to show the power of our Lord's cross, whereby, also, to every man bitten by spiritual serpents, who yet turned with an eye of faith to it, was proclaimed a cure from the bite of sin, and health for evermore?[20]

In a hymn of Lauds, we read, 'The blessed wounds of Christ are the source of universal salvation: like the brazen serpent, they heal those who have been wounded.'[21] In another, Adam of St Victor speaks of Christ as follows: 'He is this serpent that devours the serpents of Pharaoh; over Him, the malice of the dragon has no power. As the type of the brazen serpent, he heals the wounds of the fiery serpent.'[22]

An old stained glass window in the cathedral at Alençon shows the brazen serpent on a cross in the form of a T. An analogous image is to be seen at Bourges, also in a stained glass window, where the brazen serpent has become a winged dragon on the shaft of a column that extends below it to form a cross bearing the Holy Victim.

---

19. Moreover, the story of the brazen serpent forms part of a group of themes considered since the beginning of the Christian tradition, and probably in accord with the rabbinical tradition, as symbolic of the messianic truths to come: the crossing of the Red Sea, the rock, manna, the waters of Mara, the march through the desert, the column of smoke (J. Daniélou, *Sacramentum Futuri*, pp131–191).

20. Tertullian, *Against Marcion* 3, 18; 347. Cf. *Epist. of Barnabus*, 12, 6; St Cyril of Jerusalem, *Mystag. Catech.* 33, 797; St Greg. of Nyssa, *Works*, 44, 413 C–D; St Basil, *Treatise on the Holy Spirit*, 14 (PG 32, 121C); St Augustine, *Cont. Faust.* 12, 28–29 (PL 42, 269–270).

21. Hymn of Lauds, for the Feast of the Exaltation of the Cross.

22. AL, T. pasc. I, p342.

On the back of a pulpit in the church of St Pierre du Marche, at Loudun, we see a cross with a serpent coiled around it; and likewise, at St Leger (Pas-de-Calais), alongside the cross of a Calvary is coiled a serpent rising towards Jesus. It would be wrong to think that in the last two instances the serpent symbolizes the devil. In fact, here it is not a question of a serpent trampled down at the foot of the cross— a well known iconographic subject—but of a triumphant serpent that can only denote Christ. This is confirmed, moreover, by a very old Christian symbol: the Chrism arranged in such a way that it forms a T-shaped cross on which a serpent is crucified.

All of this is certainly surprising at first sight, for we are in the habit of seeing the serpent only as an evil sign, an emblem of Satan. This animal, however, is also a benefic sign, symbolizing Christ, as He himself avowed. But we know that nearly all symbols are ambivalent, and later we shall see how the ambivalence is explained in this instance. But here let us further note that the choice of the serpent as an image of Christ can be justified by gematria; in fact, the letters of the word *nahash*, meaning 'serpent' in Hebrew, have the same numerical value as the word *meshiah*, 'Messiah', 'Christ':

$$N(50) + H(8) + Sh(300) = 358$$
$$M(40) + Sh(300) + I(10) + H(8) = 358$$

In order to elucidate the symbolism of the brazen serpent, it is best not to restrict ourselves to the science of types,[23] but to appeal to the science of symbols. Typology is certainly very interesting and indispensable, for it allows us to grasp the continuity of the two Testaments and, in part, to clarify them by seeing each through the eyes of the other. But, contrary to some, we do not believe it superior to the science of symbols and to provide more profound explanations. In reality, the opposite is true. Typology is content to compare the two or three terms under consideration and to sketch an explanation which, in general, does not go beyond the historical domain; it invites us to look for the true explanation rather than providing it.

---

23. Let us remember that this is what is called the exegetical method, which consists in discovering in the Old Testament the prophetic figures of the New.

For when it is said, for example, that the brazen serpent was the 'type' of Christ, something is explained, to be sure, but not everything; in particular, it has not been said precisely why the serpent and not some other animal has been chosen to be this 'type', which is the essential point. Typology therefore needs to be deepened and explained by symbolism: the type needs to be considered not only in its biblical context, but also in its universal usage and meaning.

We shall start by completing our typology of the brazen serpent by also comparing it with the Tree of the earthly Paradise and that of the heavenly Jerusalem. Christian tradition has always associated the Cross with the Tree of Paradise, by way of saying that the Cross redressed the evil that came from the Tree. Furthermore, in traditional iconography, the serpent is shown coiled around the Tree, which leads us to the serpent coiled around a perch or staff –ultimately a tree—or crucified on the cross. The only difference is that the serpent of the earthly Paradise is not the *good* serpent, the Savior, but the angel of perdition. We easily observe that the trees of the brazen serpent and the cross, each bearing the good serpent, are inverse images of the tree of the earthly Paradise, bearing the evil serpent. This means that Christ on the tree of the Cross, as the good serpent, the brazen serpent, has healed the wounds of the satanic serpent coiled around the other tree.[24]

Further, the tree of the earthly Paradise bearing the bad serpent is the Tree of the Knowledge of Good and Evil. But there was another tree in Paradise, the Tree of Life, which was 'in the midst of the garden' (Gen. 2:9). When Adam ate the fruit of the Tree of Knowledge, he was permanently distanced from the Tree of Life and prevented from eating its fruit. Now, the Cross of Christ is also assimilated to the Tree of Life, planted at the center of the world: 'Plant immortal, it stands at the center of heaven and earth: firm upholder of the universe, bond of all things, support of the whole earth. . . .'[25] Its fruit is 'the living bread descended from heaven,' and it is also 'the heavenly

---

24. Let us note that in Mexico the serpent Quetzalcoatl is a savior god, who is offered in sacrifice for men. Another vestige of the Primordial Revelation!

25. St John Chrysostom, *Spuria*. But the attribution to St John appears quite doubtful. Text in *Homélies pascale*, I (*Sources chrétiennes* 27).

vine': 'O Cross, Tree of Life, who bore Him who is the life and ransom of the world, thou art the vine-stake from which the bunch of grapes transplanted from the vines of Engaddi is suspended.'[26] If we recall that, according to the teaching of the Fathers,[27] the Tree of the Knowledge of Good and Evil denotes sensible nature, life according to the *flesh*, whereas the Tree of Life symbolizes the intelligible world and life according to the *spirit*, the parallel between the scene of the Fall and that of the Redemption becomes remarkably clear.

The tree, in universal symbolism, denotes life and the world itself. The vertical trunk is the Axis of the World linking earth to heaven, its center. This is why it is said that the Tree of Life is at the center of Paradise. It designates more particularly the spiritual world, the world transfigured by Grace and spiritual life, like the Cross. The other tree, that of the Knowledge of Good and Evil, is in a way an illusory reflection of the first, illusory because it abuses man and distances him from life according to the spirit and from the true world. Man will neither be healed from this spiritual evil nor find immortality unless, having returned to the center of Paradise, he is able to eat from the true Tree of Life. This rediscovered tree is the Cross of Christ which restores all things to the primordial state. It is, moreover, the tree planted 'in the midst' of the heavenly Jerusalem, or paradise regained.

> In the midst of the street of it, and on either side of the river, there was the tree of life, which bare twelve manner of fruits and yielded her fruit every month: and the leaves of the tree were for the healing of the nations (Apoc. 22:2).

We can now explain the meaning of the serpent itself in these complex symbols. The serpent coiled around an axis, tree, or post embodies the spiral of Existence about the immobile Axis, image of the Supreme Principle. It is the movement of universal life, but— and this is crucial—the path of this helix can be traversed by a being either in an ascending direction towards the heavenly states, or in a

---

26. Old sequence (AL, T. pasc. II, p101).

27. For example, Maximus the Confessor and Origen (Cf. Hans Urs von Balthasar, *Cosmic Liturgy* [San Francisco: Ignatius Press, 2003], pp129 ff. and 271 ff.).

descending direction towards the infernal states.[28] The former movement is that of Redemption, symbolized by the serpent, which is Christ; the second is that of the Fall and damnation, symbolized by the serpent, which is Satan. Herein lies the explanation of the double symbolism of the serpent.

All these considerations will enable us to understand why the serpent coiled around the tree or staff is the emblem both of medicine and of Christ, savior and physician of men. At the level of bodily existence, the spiral embodied by the serpent is that of the currents of subtle and nervous life around the axis constituted by the spine, currents which, according to their sound functioning and balance, condition health.[29] This is the aspect of the spiral that is represented by the staff of Aesculapius, as the emblem of medicine, the role of which is to act upon the vital forces without, however, losing sight of its relationship with the higher meaning of the symbol. The latter belongs essentially to Christ as the universal Word and master of life. On the other hand, 'as the supreme Priest, He is the one true physician' hailed by the inscription at Timgad, physician of souls and bodies, of the whole man.

And if medicine is generally the prerogative of the priesthood, participating in the priesthood of Christ, this accounts for healing being a sign of the mission of the Apostles. 'Behold the miracles that will accompany all those who have believed. . . . They will lay their hands on the sick and they shall be healed' (Mark 16:17–18). Thus St Peter cured a lame man in the name of Jesus of Nazareth (Acts 3:6). In principle, the priest assures the health of men, as he does the wellbeing of vegetation. As a result of changes in the conditions of existence of our world, conditions essentially linked to times and places, and about which we need not go into detail here, the power to heal sicknesses is no longer effective in the priesthood.[30] It occurs

---

28. On this subject, see R. Guénon, *Symbolism of the Cross*, p 54 ff. and p 123 ff.

29. This can be clearly seen in a traditional medicine like Chinese acupuncture.

30. Until rather recently it was manifested among the kings of France, whose royalty had a distinctly priestly character. On this subject see Marc Bloch, *Les Rois thaumaturges* (passim) and P. Gordon, *Le Sacerdoce à travers les âges*, pp 28–31. (This book contains very interesting information, but is spoiled by a more than contestable general argument.)

only sporadically among certain saints, but then they heal only in their personal capacity, through a personal grace, and not by virtue of the priestly function. We should not forget, however, that the Sacrament of Holy Unction sometimes effects unexpected cures, *where there is faith.*

On the other hand, the Divine medicine works in a regular and normal way at certain privileged centers, located near certain sanctuaries, as at Lourdes, where the power of Christ, *medicus omnipotens,* is manifested through the Divine Mother. Lourdes is like a living chapter of the Gospel: there, because one believes, one is healed, and the bodily cures that happen are often, as ever, the prelude to more marvelous cures of the soul. There, Christ can be clearly seen in His complementary roles of savior and physician, *soter* and *iatros.*

3

The
Warrior God

THE EXPRESSION 'Lord of hosts', *Deus sabaoth*, is found through-out the Old Testament, where God appears as a warrior prince, the champion of His people in the face of their enemies. It has remained alive in the New Testament where, in a certain manner, it is applied to Christ Himself, and where, moreover, a military conception of life and salvation is developed, in which the warrior symbolism strikingly conveys the profound nature of Christian morality and spirituality.

God is presented as a warlord defending Israel in innumerable passages of the Old Testament: 'The Lord of hosts is with us; the God of Jacob is our refuge' (Psalm 45); 'He has set His camp in the midst of His people, to deliver us from the hand of all our enemies' (Jth. 16:4). Champion of the people, God is also champion of the king who asks His aid against his enemies: 'Arise, O Lord, disappoint him and supplant him: deliver my soul from the wicked one; thy sword from the enemies of thy hand. O Lord, divide them from the few of the earth in their life' (Psalm 16). 'Plead my cause, O Lord, with them that strive with me: fight against them that fight against me. Take hold of shield and buckler, and stand up for my help. Draw out also the spear, and stop the way against them that persecute me' (Psalm 34).

It is God who gives victory and, if Israel suffers a defeat, it is because God has not supported her: 'O God, thou hast cast us off, thou hast scattered us. Thou hast been displeased' (Psalm 59). Many

passages from Exodus, Deuteronomy, and the Psalms offer us striking pictures of the Divine Warrior furthering the saga of Israel:

> The Lord is a man of war: the Lord is His name. Pharaoh's chari-
> ots and his host hath He cast into the sea: his chosen captains
> also are drowned in the Red Sea. . . . Thou hast overthrown them
> that rose up against thee: Thou sentest forth Thy wrath, which
> consumed them as stubble (Song of Moses, Exod. 15:3–7).

> The chariots of God are twenty thousand, even thousands of
> angels: the Lord is among them, as in Sinai, in the holy place.
> Thou hast ascended on high, Thou hast led captivity captive
> (Psalm 67).

In Habakkuk we find the following extraordinary martial ode, its
splendid and fierce poetry remains unmatched:

> God came from the south, and the Holy One from mount Pha-
> ran; his glory covered the heavens, and the earth was full of his
> praise. His brightness was as the light, rays flashed from his
> hands... Death went before his face, and the exterminating angel
> went before his feet. He stood, and measured the earth; he
> looked and shook the nations; and the everlasting mountains
> were scattered. . . . O God who, to save thy people, mounted
> upon thy horses and thy chariots, thou armed thyself with thy
> bow: thou hast fulfilled thy promises to the tribes. . . . The sun
> and the moon stood still in their habitation at the light of thy
> arrows as they sped, at the flash of thy glittering spear. Thou
> didst bestride the earth in fury, thou didst trample the nations in
> anger. . . . Thou didst crush the head of the wicked, who came
> like a whirlwind to scatter me. . . . Thou didst trample the sea
> with thy horses, the surging of mighty waters (Hab. 3:3 ff.).

Elsewhere, we have the terrifying celestial warrior, armed with
lightning and riding upon the clouds:

> If I whet my glittering sword, and my hand take hold on judg-
> ment; I will render vengeance to my enemies, and will reward
> them that hate me. I will make my arrows drunk with blood, and
> my sword shall devour flesh; and that with the blood of the slain

and of the captives, from the beginning of revenges upon the enemy (Song of Moses, Deut. 3:41–42).

These fearsome deeds of the Divine Warrior are explained by the fact that he is king, a feared king, establishing respect for the right and punishing offenders as an example, for according to the traditional adage, *gladius legis custos*: the sword is the guardian of the law. 'The king's strength also loveth judgment; thou dost establish equity' (Psalm 98). 'Say among the heathen that the Lord reigneth: he shall judge the people righteously' (Psalm 95). 'His eyes behold the nations: let not the rebellious exalt themselves' (Psalm 65). 'Clouds and darkness are round about him: righteousness and judgment are the habitation of his throne. A fire goeth before him, and burneth up his enemies round about. . . .' (Psalm 96); see also Job 36:32–3 and 37:1–4).

But, it will be said, this is a conception belonging to the Old Testament, which has been superseded by Christianity, the religion of peace, in which Christ is opposed to the warrior God of the Israelites.

This is a bit hasty, though. To be sure, during His life on earth Christ preached a religion of peace and love, which was profoundly different from ancient Judaism. But we should not go too far. In truth, it is sheer folly to speak of Jesus as a pacifist, as is the tendency today, and even, sometimes, a socialist. It is to forget that St Paul called Him the 'Mighty God', and that in the Gospel He said, 'I came not to send peace but a sword.' It is above all to forget Christ, the Judge of the Apocalypse. Here He appears in the guise of a warrior of gigantic proportions, a cosmic warrior engaged in a universal battle, the struggle of Light against Darkness. The Old Testament was already familiar with this cosmic warrior who sometimes represented Time and its inexorable passage, Time that kills, and sometimes the vanquisher of the monster Rahab.

For a thousand years in thy sight are but as yesterday when it is past, and as a watch in the night. Thou carriest them away as with a flood. . . . For we are consumed by thine anger, and by thy wrath are we troubled. . . . For all our days are passed away in thy wrath; we spend our years as a tale that is told.... (Psalm 89). I kill and I make alive; I wound and I heal' (Deut. 32:39).

There is, moreover, a curious analogy between the terms employed in these biblical passages and those of the Bhagavad Gita, where God says, 'I am the Spirit of Time, destroyer of the world, come forth for the destruction of peoples' (*Bhagavad Gita* 11, 32).

In other places in the Bible, God is the warrior who kills Rahab, the mythical monster representing chaos. Here warfare represents creation itself as a struggle, and finally the triumph, of order against the disorder of original Chaos. (War, moreover, is justified to the extent that it aims at eliminating a disorder and reestablishing the order demanded by the law of creation):

Thou rulest the raging of the sea [symbol of the chaotic powers]: when the waves thereof arise, thou stillest them. Thou hast broken Rahab in pieces, as one that is slain; thou hast scattered thine enemies with thy strong arm (Psalm 88, cf. Psalm 103, Isa. 51:9).

The image of the heavenly warrior slaying the monster is to be found in India: Indra blasting Vrita with lightning, and in Greece: Apollo transfixing Python. Apollo is the archer who shoots the solar arrows, alongside Zeus striking the Titans with lightning. There are thus two series of parallel symbols connected, in the one case, with the rays of the sun and, in the other, with lightning, as in the biblical texts cited above.[1] We are in the presence of a symbolical context that is not only well-defined, but found everywhere.[2]

At the beginning of the Apocalypse, Christ comes forth terrifyingly. His eyes are like flames, His feet like burning brass, His voice like the roar of flooding water, His face like the sun, and from His

---

1. Lightning and the solar ray are the archetypes of traditional weapons. In connection with this, see R. Guénon, *Symbols of Sacred Science*, tr. H.D. Fohr (Hillsdale, NY: Sophia Perennis, 2001), pp167–184.

2. M. Eliade, *Patterns in Comparative Religion*, tr. Rosemary Sheed (NY: Sheed & Ward. 1958), chaps. 2 and 3 — On the correspondences between Christ and the solar Apollo, see our book, *The Symbolism of the Christian Temple*, pp134–138. Some Italian miniatures of the twelfth century show God as an archer hunting man in paradise, for example (Didron, *Christian Iconography*, vol. 1, tr. E.J. Millington [NY: Frederick Ungar Publishing Co., 1965], p186).

mouth there comes forth a two-edged sword (1:13–16). Further on, St John sees a white horse advancing, 'and he that sat on him had a bow; a crown was given unto him; and he went forth conquering, and to conquer' (6:2).

After Michael and his angels have fought against the Dragon (12:7–12), it is the triumphant Christ who advances on a white horse, clothed in purple, and with a crown upon his head

> With justice doth he judge and fight. . . . And the armies that are in heaven followed him on white horses. . . . And out of his mouth proceedeth a sharp sword, that with it he should smite the nations.

This vision of Christ as a triumphant *imperator* is a frequent theme of ancient iconography. For example, it is seen in a fresco at Auxerre (in the crypt of St Etienne) and on a Byzantine medal in the Strasbourg Museum, which shows Christ on horseback striking down the Dragon with His lance.

This battle against the Dragon is not only the task of St Michael and Christ, it is the very life of the Christian and the Church. Indeed, from the beginning both have been compared to a militia, the community of the faithful on earth being the *Church Militant*, and the community of saints in heaven, the *Church Triumphant*. Christ is the emperor, the *imperator*, the supreme commander of His disciples; the faithful are *cohorts* triumphing over the demons; sanctuaries are *camps*, the cross is a *standard* (cf. the hymn *Vexilla regis* of Good Friday); baptism is compared to an oath of fidelity; the practices of piety to *drills* and *sentry-duty*; apostates are *deserters*; finally, the vanquisher of demons is *crowned* like a victor.[3] The essential themes of this militant life are already present in St Paul: 'Thou therefore endure hardness, as a good soldier of Christ' (2 Tim. 2:3). 'Let us therefore cast off the works of darkness, and let us put on the armor of light' (Rom. 13:12).

---

3. F. Cumont, *The Oriental Religions in Roman Paganism* (Chicago: Open Court Publishing Company, 1911), p xix.

Therefore take unto you the armor of God, that you may be able to resist in the evil day, and to stand in all things perfect. Stand therefore, having your loins girt about with truth, and having on the breastplate of justice, and your feet shod with the preparation of the gospel of peace: In all things taking the shield of faith, wherewith you may be able to extinguish all the fiery darts of the most wicked one. And take unto you the helmet of salvation, and the sword of the Spirit (which is the word of God) (Eph. 6: 13–17). And if a man also strive for masteries, yet is he not crowned, except he strive lawfully (2 Tim. 2:5).

Likewise, St Leo, referring to Christ's battle in the wilderness against the devil and his temptations, writes: 'If Christ fought, it was so that we also, in our turn, might fight. If he conquered, it was so that we also might gain the victory.'[4] And he compares Lent to a period of military exercises: the Christian, as a good soldier of Christ, should submit to the discipline of the virtues.[5]

But the Christian's battle for the Heavenly City is not only situated on the spiritual plane; he can also be induced to fight for the earthly city. War, on earth, is nothing but the reflection of the heavenly battle of Light against Darkness, of Christ against the Serpent. A Christian can be sanctified through the sword in a just war. For proof, we have the existence of the institution of chivalry and the pure figures of St Louis and St Joan of Arc. For patrons, chivalry had St Michael, the heavenly warrior, and St George, who was also represented as crushing the Dragon in order to deliver a princess on the point of being devoured.[6] This means that in war and on the earthly plane the earthly knight, the Christian soldier, occupies the place of the angels, the heavenly cavalry surrounding Christ in the struggle against Evil. In light of these considerations, we are able to justify not only the profession of arms, but also envisage a spirituality of warfare, which is what chivalry embodied. This is a good example of the sacralization of an occupation by referring it to a heavenly model.

4. *Serm.* 39, 3
5. Ibid. and *Serm*, 41.1.
6. On this subject, a certain continuity is to be seen between the two Testaments in the fact that St Michael, who was the protecting angel of Israel, became so for the Church (Hymn of Vespers, 8 May).

4

The
Divine Potter

THE REPRESENTATION of God the Creator as a potter molding the world and man after the manner of a pot, or, according to a variant, as a sculptor fashioning a statue, goes back to the most distant past and is to be found nearly everywhere. This is easy to explain, for the action of the one who molds is one of the most primordial, at least where a civilization is manifested. According to G. Duhamel, 'No occupation reminds us more of God, of this God who forms man from the dust of the earth.'[1]

Thus, at Memphis, the god Ptah, patron of arts and creator god, whose name no doubt meant 'the sculptor', worked on a wheel. But the Egyptian demiurge par excellence was the god of Elephantine, Khnoum; he too was a potter. On his wheel he fashioned everything that was created: the pot, the cosmic egg containing all creatures, and the human embryo. The following are examples of how his praises were sung: 'He is the Master of the Wheel'; 'he fashions men on the wheel'; 'the wheel is in front of him, his two hands are busy molding, his fingers separate the limbs (from the lump),' 'You are the almighty. . . . You have made man. On your wheel you have formed livestock large and small, you have formed all things on your wheel.'[2]

1. G. Duhamel, *Le Prince Jaffar.*
2. In *Naissance du monde,* pp73–74.

In a related sphere, 'the Molder' is a fairly widespread divine name among a variety of African tribes.[3]

This is exactly the sense of the Greek *plastes*, the agent noun from the verb *plasso* (to mold), that Philo of Alexandria used to designate the creator god.[4] In doing so, moreover, Philo showed himself the faithful heir of all Hellenism where, in the Timaeus, Plato has the Demiurge ordering the inferior gods to 'mold perishable bodies.'[5] The illustrious disciple of Socrates was only repeating the lesson of the Greek religious tradition, which, in the two myths of the birth of Pandora and the appearance of the new humanity after the flood, presents the creation of man as a process of molding. In the first, we see Zeus ordering Hephaestus to create Pandora by first soaking the earth, then by breathing into it the voice and energies of a human being, and shaping it into the body of a virgin after the likeness of the immortal goddesses.[6] In the second, Zeus, after the flood that had drowned humanity, ordered Prometheus and Athena to fashion in like manner human figures of clay, reserving to himself the task of breathing life into them.[7]

In this we recognize the pattern of the Biblical account, which says that 'the Lord formed man of the dust of the ground' (Gen. 2:7). The Marian liturgy, too, says, 'Hail to thee, Mary, who, remaining virgin, became the mother of the Potter who fashioned Adam from the dust of the earth.'[8] And the image of the divine *Plastes* is found in

---

3. P. Fournier, *Hist. d. religions non-chrétiennes*, p 46.

4. Philo, *De opif. mundi*, 434

5. *Timaeus* 42D. — Moreover, this plastic symbolism underlies the conception of the Platonic demiurge. See e.g., 27D–29D. And Proclus, in his commentary on this dialogue, compares the demiurge to Phidias (*In Tim.* 84D).

6. Hesiod, *Works and Days*, 60.

7. Aesop, *Fables* 153 and 183; Philemon, *Frag. comic. graec.* IV, 32 (Meineke); Callim., *Frag.* 87; Lucian, *Dialogue of the Gods* I,1. The image of the potter god is found again among the Stoics (Epict. 1, 1, 7; 2, 665; 4, 1, 549, and 556; Marcus Aurelius 7, 23) and in John Chrysostom, *Or.* 19, 51

8. 'Hymn to the Virgin', in M. Hayek, *Liturgie maronite*, p 245. The following stanza of this hymn develops another artisanal image: 'Hail to thee, Mary, who, remaining virgin, became the mother of the Painter who drew Eve and gave her to Adam.' The image of the Divine Painter is also found in a vision of St Margaret Mary Alacoque.

other books of Holy Scripture, where God is the modeler of both the world and man: 'The sea is his and he made it; and his hands formed the dry land' (Psalm 94). But what the Lord particularly reserves to Himself is the molding of the heart of man, the center of his being, the shape of which is comparable to an ovoidal hemisphere and recalls the egg fashioned by Khnoum on his wheel: 'He fashioneth the hearts of them all' (Psalm 32). We shall soon see the development that this theme subsequently underwent. Meanwhile, let us again take note of the word used by the Psalmist to express the omnipotence of God over man: what, in fact, could be more expressive of the total dependence and nothingness proper to man in relation to his Lord, than to compare the former to the vessel of earth that the potter, judging it to be imperfect, rejects: 'Thou shalt break them with a rod of iron; thou shalt dash them in pieces like a potter's vessel' (Psalm 2:9).[9]

It is in Ecclesiasticus and Jeremiah that the image of the Divine Potter assumes all its fullness. The author of Ecclesiasticus pauses a moment to watch the potter at work and gives us a graphic portrait of him, a sort of generic picture and a rather rare passage in sacred literature:

> So doth the potter sitting at his work, turning the wheel about with his feet, who is always carefully set to his work, and maketh all his work by number. He fashioneth the clay with his arm, and boweth down his strength before his feet (Eccles. 38:32–33).

This care, this skill, this freedom of the human artist before his work, perfectly evokes the attitude of the Divine Artist vis-à-vis His creature:

> All men are from the ground, and out of the earth, from whence Adam was created. As the potter's clay is in his hand, to fashion and order it: all his ways are according to his ordering: so man is in the hand of him that made him, and he will render to him according to his judgment (ibid., 33:10, 13–14).

---

9. Seneca, too, said: 'What is man? A vessel that breaks at the slightest knock, at the least movement' (*Ad Marc de consolatione* II, 3).

The image, which we find again in Job 10:8–9: ('Thine hands have made me and fashioned me.... Remember, I beseech thee, that thou hast made me as the clay'), has passed into the poetry of the liturgy. Thus, as we have seen, a hymn of the Syrian churches addresses the Virgin as follows: 'Hail to thee, Mary, who, remaining virgin, became the mother of the Potter who fashioned Adam from the dust of the earth' (M. Hayek, *Liturgie maronite*, 245).

In Jeremiah, we find the same theme as in Ecclesiasticus:

The word which came to Jeremiah from the Lord, saying, arise, and go down to the potter's house, and there I will cause thee to hear my words. Then I went down to the potter's house, and, behold he wrought a work on the wheel. And the vessel that he made from clay was marred in the hand of the potter: so he made it again another vessel, as seemed good to the potter to make it. Then the word of the Lord came to me saying, O house of Israel, cannot I do with you as this potter? Saith the Lord. Behold, as the clay is in the potter's hand, so are ye in mine hand, O house of Israel (Jer. 18:1–6).

The symbolism is perhaps even more telling in Isaiah: 'Thus saith the Lord, the Holy One of Israel, and his Potter' (45:11); 'But now, O Lord, thou art our father; we are the clay, and thou our potter; and we all are the work of thy hands' (64:8); 'Woe unto him that striveth with his Maker; let the potsherd strive with the potsherds of the earth. Shall the clay say to him that shapeth it, What makest thou?' (45:9). And is it not the echo of these prophets and sages that we hear again, at the dawn of Christianity, in these words of St Paul: 'O man, who art thou that repliest against God? Shall the thing formed say to him that formed it, Why hast thou made me thus?' (Rom. 9:20).

These beautiful literary passages, filled with the solemn accents of inspired writers, were born from meditation on the potter at work. As with the Apostle, the prophets of Israel, and the sages of Greece and Egypt, meditation on the image of the potter can still convey its sublime message to us as well.

To understand its full import, we must first grasp the phenomenology of modeling gestures, their appearance and sequence from the stage of the lump of unformed clay thrown onto the wheel, to the perfecting of the work. This phenomenology, however, is not enough in itself, being but the means of acceding to a higher knowledge. It is necessary to pass from the phenomenology to the ontology of a movement, to its profound significance, to its essence, the foundation of its symbolism.

We can think of no better introduction to a phenomenology of modeling gestures than to quote G. Duhamel cited at the beginning of this chapter, who was inspired by the spectacle of the famous potters of Jerba. We shall observe how he was able to capture the beauty and sanctity of the act of modeling:

> When the soft, stone-free roll is placed on the small wheel, Yamun springs lightly to his place. He murmurs the humble prayer sanctifying every need—In the Name of God!—and the mystery begins. It is the beginning of the world.... Yamun imparts a circular movement to the apparatus, the movement of the stars, the principle of all genesis.... An earthen flower rises, rises and opens, although he scarcely seems to touch it. He follows it in its ascension, caresses it, and restrains it with awe. Like a god, Yamun concentrates on his work, and suddenly it is finished. With a single stroke of the wire, he detaches it from the socle. An offering! With careful hands, he holds it up. Is it real? It has risen so quickly from the original ground, that we might believe that simply dreaming it was enough to make it.

In this description we already perceive the outline of an ontology of the modeling gesture. When the author compares the making of the pot to the 'beginning of the world', he situates it exactly within the spiritual perspective that defines it in depth.

At its own level, the gesture of molding reproduces in a particularly striking way the process of creation, which is defined ontologically as the descent of form into matter, the imprinting of the essence upon substance. At the highest level, it is the Divine Spirit who 'descends' upon Prime Matter, or Universal Substance. The latter is a 'chaos', which He orders according to His Law or Wisdom,

His Holy Wisdom, in order to transform it into a 'cosmos', that is to say, an ordered and harmonious world. The same applies to man, constituted from 'dust', which the 'breath' of the Divine Spirit comes to animate, and to all creatures. This is why God as creator is called *dator formarum*, 'giver of form', the latter word needing to be understood in the philosophical sense which naturally goes beyond the concept of visible or material form, and designates the whole nature of the being under consideration.

On a lower level, the artisan's gestures are a reflection of this divine activity, and are like its continuation, whether it be the gestures of the quarryman, the potter or any other artisan. In the case of the quarryman, the rough stone plays the role of prime matter or substance, which the hand of man cuts according to the form he has in his mind, which is thereby made to 'descend' upon it. The same applies to the mass of clay molded by the potter. Here the gestures are perhaps even more suggestive than those of the stonemason, for, as Duhamel rightly noted, they reproduce 'the circular movement, the movement of the stars, the principle of all genesis.' Under the impulse imparted to the wheel by the artisan, the mass of earth is lifted around an empty center, which is the axis that governs the gyration and conditions the structure of the entire form. In all traditional civilizations, this axis—like that which governs the construction of the temple[10]—is consciously identified with the axis of the world, the cosmic image of the Divine Principle, of the unmoved mover, likewise invisible, which is the very root of the transformation of Chaos into Cosmos. The relating of the particular action/gesture to the Primordial Action/Gesture confers on the former its sacredness, and in this way it becomes a support of meditation for the artisan, as in this Hindu potter's song:

> O my heart, do not take after the wheel, but be equal to its center, which keeps itself at rest. If the wheel turns so vigorously, it is because its center remains motionless.[11]

10. On this subject, see our book, *The Symbolism of the Christian Temple* (pp 83–92).

11. D.G. Mukerji, *Brahmane et Pariah*, p114. Cf. the jade ritual *pi*, its flat disc pierced with a central hole representing the 'emptiness of the hub that lets the wheel turn' (P. Grison, *Notes sur le Jade*, in *Études Traditionnelles*, 382, 1964, 69 and 74).

To conclude, we have a text from St Irenaeus, which, presented as a gloss of Ecclesiasticus, transposes the symbolism of the Divine Potter from the cosmological to the mystical plane.

If, then, thou art God's workmanship, await the hand of thy Maker which creates everything in due time; in due time as far as thou art concerned, whose creation is being carried out. Offer to Him thy heart in a soft and tractable state, and preserve the form in which the Creator has fashioned thee, having moisture in thyself, lest, by becoming hardened, thou lose the impressions of His fingers. But by preserving the framework thou shalt ascend to that which is perfect, for the moist clay which is in thee is hidden [there] by the workmanship of God. His hand fashioned thy substance; He will cover thee over [too] within and without with pure gold and silver, and He will adorn thee to such a degree, that even 'the King Himself shall have pleasure in thy beauty'. . . . For creation is an attribute of the goodness of God but to be created is that of human nature. If then, thou shalt deliver up to Him what is thine, that is, faith towards Him and subjection, thou shalt receive His handiwork, and shall be a perfect work of God.[12]

12. St Irenaeus, *Contra haer.* IV, 39, 2.

5

God
the Weaver

THE FIGURE of the potter seems to us an especially appropriate way of representing the Divine Activity, which, together with its immediate comprehensibility, explains its wide distribution. However, let it be said once again that every artisanal occupation is capable of evoking this activity, since it is its normal prolongation, provided it is natural, that is to say, aims at satisfying the natural needs of man by equally natural means. And this applies to another symbol of the divine activity: the work of weaving.

Weaving serves to designate creation under all its aspects, beginning with the creation of man.

Sometimes existence is compared to a thread. We have only to think of expressions like 'the thread of time', 'the thread of life', or 'life holding on by a thread', or recall the familiar image of the Fates, 'the sad spinsters',[1] or remember Claudian addressing the god of the dead as follows: 'O omnipotent judge of the night, ruler of the shades, for whom the thread of our spindle labors....'[2] Sometimes it is creatures, and man in particular, that are compared to a cloth woven by the divinity: 'The gods chain souls in bodies when they weave living creatures,' wrote Olympiodorus,[3] following Plato, who spoke of a 'mortal part of the soul woven by the gods on the immortal

---

1. *Odyssey*, 7, 198.
2. Claudian, *De raptu Proserpinae* I, 55–56.
3. Olympiodorus, *in Phaed.* (Norvin, p88).

part.'[4] The same idea occurs in India: 'The Breath (creator) wove human life,'[5] while for Marcus Aurelius, meditating on the destiny of man, 'bodies are of mud and bone, an interlaced network of nerves, veins and arteries. . . .'

The stoic philosopher compared not only man's body, but also his individual destiny and the total harmony of the world enclosing him, to weaving:

All that happens to you was destined from the beginning, by order of the whole, and was woven there. . . . Willingly give thyself up to Clotho, one of the Fates, allowing her to spin thy thread into whatever things she pleases. . . . . Consider . . . in what way things are woven and coiled together. . . . Reflect often upon the interconnectedness of all things in the world and the relationship of one to another. In a certain sense, they are all woven together, and are consequently all friends one of another. One indeed is chained to the other, as a result of ordained movement, of common inspiration, and of the unity of substance.

In passing, it will have been noticed how this last thought of Marcus Aurelius, by recalling the creative breath, ties in with the Hindu text cited above.[6]

Thus, not only are individuals viewed as products of weaving, but the entire creation, the cosmos, is an immense cloth woven by God. It is noteworthy, in this regard, that the patronesses of weaving, such as the Egyptian Neith, Athena, and Proserpine, are also goddesses of cosmic or chthonic nature. According to Porphyry,

the body is a garment with which the soul is invested. . . . Thus according to Orpheus, Proserpine, who presides over every thing generated from seed, is represented weaving a web; and the

---

4. Plato, *Timaeus* 41D. Cf. Proclus, *In Timae.*, 310–11.

5. *Atharva-Veda*, x, 2, 13.

6. Marcus Aurelius, *Meditations*, II, 2; 4, 26 and 34; 4, 40; 6, 38. Cf. also 3, 16; 7, 9, and 10, 5. Likewise Proclus tells us that Circe presides over generation: to be born, he says, is for a soul to see woven about itself, like a cocoon around a silkworm, the networks of nerves, veins, and arteries, and the whole web of flesh that will constitute the body (Proclus, *In Cra.* 22, 7ff.).

ancients called heaven by the name of 'peplos', which is as it were the veil or tegument of the celestial gods.[7]

The Upanishads teach that the supreme Brahma is 'That upon which the worlds are woven as warp and woof'; and, again, 'The (divine) Air has woven the universe by binding together, as with a thread this world and the next and all beings.'[8] This image of the universal thread is found in Babylonian mythology, where *Markasu* is the cosmic principle uniting things.[9] In China, the Tao or the Way, that is to say the metaphysical principles and their knowledge, is called 'the warp of all creation.'[10]

> To adhere strictly to the way of the ancient tradition ... is not only to have in one's hand all the threads of present existence, but to possess all the elements of the current cycle .., to know the beginning of tradition, the principles, the primordial origins whence all flows; this is what is called the warp and the woof of the Way, its reflection, its unwinding.[11]

Here we are a long way from the somewhat meager image of the Fates; we are witness to the grand spectacle of the Divinity weaving the universe on a cosmic loom. The *Tao Te Ching* presents Universal Existence as issuing from the double movement of divine Energy in its two aspects, active and passive, *yang* and *yin*. According to commentators, this movement is 'the to and fro of the shuttle on the cosmic loom.'[12]

The Bible does not offer such vast panoramas embracing the fullness of creation, because it is first and foremost centered on man, and is primarily interested in the latter's personal relations with God rather than cosmology and metaphysics properly so-called.

---

7. Porphyry, *On the Cave of the Nymphs*, 14.

8. *Mundaka Up.* 2, 2, 5; *Brihad Aranyaka Up.* 3, 8, 7–8 (cited in R. Guénon, *The Symbolism of the Cross*, tr. Angus Macnab (Ghent, NY: Sophia Perennis, 2001), chap. 14 ('The Symbolism of Weaving').

9. M. Eliade, 'The "God who Binds"' in *Images and Symbols*, tr. P. Mairet (Princeton, NJ: Princeton University Press, 1991), p115.

10. Ibid.

11. *Tao Te Ching*, XIV, Fr. tr. J. Leonnet, in ET 364 (1961), pp79–80.

12. Chang-Hung-Yang, cited in R. Guénon, op.cit., p77.

Even in this regard, however, impressive images of the Weaver God are to be found therein. The psalmist says to the Lord, 'Thou hast formed my reins and woven me in my mother's womb' (Psalm 138). Job says, 'From bone and sinew hast thou woven me,' (10:11) and again, 'My days are swifter than a weaver's shuttle, and are spent without hope'(7:6). The same tone is heard in Ezechias: 'My life is cut off, as by a weaver: whilst I was yet but beginning, he cut me off. From morning even to night thou wilt make an end of me' (Isaiah 38:12).

All cloth is essentially composed of the interweaving of vertical fixed threads, the warp, with horizontal moving threads, the woof. Now this structure has its model in nature, where all is as it were woven by the divine Artisan. The example of the human body was cited above; we shall consider two additional examples, the tree and the spider.

The tree is a woven tissue. The fibers and vessels, rising from the earth to its summit, constitute its warp, and the living substance, which gathers around the fibers and the vessels, its woof. The same structure is found in the vegetable parts, too, for example, in the leaves.

The case of the spider is even more striking. Its web is the most perfect natural model of weaving. Here, the radial threads of the circle constitute the warp and the concentric threads the woof. This structure may seem different from that of cloth, since it is circular, but to see its analogy with ordinary weaving it suffices to consider the center of the web as infinitely distant: the radii then become parallel vertical lines, and the circumference and inner concentric circles, straight lines perpendicular to these radii, and therefore horizontal. What is amazing is that, in weaving, the spider proceeds in the same way as man. Thus, the diadem spider, *Epeira diadema*,[13] first erects the radii (the warp) on a frame of thread; then upon these radii she as it were 'positions' a spiral with a central dwelling

---

13. What follows on the Epeira is based on M. Sire, *L'intelligence des animaux* (1956). See also A. Tilqin, *La Toile géométrique des araignées*, 1942.

space. The observations of naturalists have shown this spiral to have a remarkable feature: it is a logarithmic spiral, that is to say it is defined by a geometric progression related to the golden number. Let us open a parenthesis here. The golden number is a relationship that, as we know through Ghyka's work in particular, regulates the harmonious growth of living beings and correctly understood architectural proportions alike. It is the number that permits the creation of harmonious order. In light of this, it is astonishing to read this conclusion from the pen of the author cited above:

So much care and precision [on the part of the spider] is exercised in pure futility. . . . All webs hold the insects that fall into them, whatever their structure and geometrical aspect! . . .

Few words, much nonsense! Proof that erudition can exist side by side with metaphysical ignorance. . . . As if the harmonious character of the diadem's web was not the signature—how eloquent—of Him who, according to Scripture 'has made all things by number, weight, and measure!

Far more metaphysically profound than our scholars are the people who, faced with the spectacle of the insect weaver, have seen in it an image of God weaving the world. Such are the Ahom of the Far East, who believe in the existence of a cosmic spider created by God that has woven the web of heaven.[14] The latter expression, as will have been observed, is altogether analogous to that of the ancient Greeks; according to Porphyry, 'Heaven is a peplos' (see above).

The expression is also found in India: 'The weaver of the web of the world is certainly he who shines yonder (the Sun), for he moves along these worlds as if upon a web.'[15] And again: 'The unique God, like a spider, envelops himself in threads issued from primordial Matter.'[16]

The spider's web can all the more be taken as a symbol of the

---

14. Ch. Archainbault, *La naissance du monde selon les traditions Lao* in *Naissnace du Monde*, p385.

15. *Satapatha Brahmana*, 14, 2, 2, 22.

16. *Pradhana Upanishad*, 6, 10.

world in that its circular form may be seen as a cut made in the cosmogonic spheroid, just as the logarithmic spiral corresponds exactly to the plane projection of the spiral movement defining the deployment of universal Life. The spider can, with reason, even be chosen as a symbol of the divinity in that it makes its web from its own substance, just as God creates the world, not from His Substance, certainly, but from the Ideas and according to the archetype contained in His Mind.[17]

Like that of the potter, the act of the weaver is well suited to recall the Primordial Act creating the world, while the cloth calls to mind creation itself.

Cloth, we have said, is defined by its warp and woof. The threads of the warp are fixed and straight, thereby symbolizing the fixed element, the principles and laws of the world, being. The threads of the woof are mobile and entwined, and thus clearly represent the variable and contingent element, the event, the individual, becoming. Also, it will be noticed that the fundamental structure of cloth, constituted by a warp and a woof crossing each other perpendicularly, reproduces the form of the cross. In the latter, the vertical axis is, as it were, celestial, linking the earth to heaven, whereas the horizontal branch is, rather, terrestrial, symbolizing the extension of the world and beings.

The warp therefore represents the principles, between them linking the worlds and states of being. And each thread of the warp links the corresponding points in the different states. The woof, in its turn, symbolizes the ensemble of events taking place in each world, and each thread the unfolding of events in a given world. Or again: the manifestation of a being within a state of existence, as an event, is determined by the meeting of a vertical and a horizontal thread. The vertical thread is the being in its essence; the horizontal, crossed by the vertical, is the determined state of existence. Their intersection determines the relations of the being in question with the cosmic

17. This symbolism exists in India. See the commentary of Shankaracharya on the *Brahma-Sutras* in Guénon, op. cit., p78.

milieu surrounding it. For example, the individual nature of a man is the meeting of these two threads.[18]

To conclude, let us say that the phases of weaving, like those of the potter's work, wondrously recall the process of creation as the latter issues from the hands of God. The weaver is initially faced with a pile of loose threads, as the potter is with a heap of clay. This shapeless matter recalls the primordial Chaos, that is to say the ensemble of possibilities of being and existence not yet distinguished in the mind of the divine Artisan. The human artisan then separates the threads, and places them one by one in order, each according to where it will fit into the composition of the cloth, just as the potter shapes his clay and imprints upon it the form of the pot. This is the phase of the passage from the unformed to the formed, under the impetus of the spirit, which, impregnated with the form, creates the object. It does this in imitation of the Spirit of God who, moving upon the Waters, that is to say Chaos, divides them and separates the elements in order to arrange them with a view to making a Cosmos of them. That is to say, an Order, a work where the *spirit* has descended into a *matter*. And the condition making this order possible in the case of both weaving and potting will have been noted: it is the vertical axis, the *empty center* about which the clay turns on the wheel, the threads of the warp about which those of the woof wind. These are humble symbols of the universal polar Axis about which the movement of the world takes place and which itself is the cosmic reflection of the Unmoved Mover. Around the vertical threads of the warp, the weaver runs, winds and knots the horizontal threads; likewise, on the Cosmic Loom the Divine Weaver winds and twists the threads of existence, of beings and events, and thus, bit by bit, weaves the fabric of the world and of history. Finally, when all the threads in the pile have been used up, that is to say when all the possibilities of existence have found their place and played their role in the cloth, the cosmic Loom will be stopped. The Divine Artisan, the Logos, will detach the finished cloth and offer it to His Father, and, His work accomplished, will repose in the eternal Sabbath (Gen. 2:1).

18. Guénon, ibid., p79.

6

God
the Architect
and Mason

THE WORK of the architect or mason—they are one and the same in traditional civilizations—is just as essential to human life as that of the weaver, and more so than that of the potter. Like the other two, it also is related to God. In the idea of God as architect and mason we have a universal and more especially biblical theme that has been widely developed: God is the architect of the house, the universe and, finally, the Church.

The idea that God is the author of all construction is based on passages from Scripture such as this: 'Except the Lord build the house, they labor in vain that build it. *Nisi Dominus aedificaverit domum*' (Psalm 126). Such a saying implies, moreover, that God is not only the architect of the house but that He is the *only* architect. We can consider it as a specific application of the Scholastic adage: 'God is the sole Artisan,' *Unus artifex est Deus*, who is able to assume various forms according to the different 'arts'. We shall cite only one example of this—relating to the profession of arms—provided by the famous saying of Joan of Arc: 'Men will battle and God will give the victory,' which exactly corresponds to the saying that Abu-l-Hashash had carved, even to the point of obsession, on the walls of his palace at Granada: 'God alone is the conqueror,' *la ghalib illa 'Llah*. Such words remind us of the saying of Christ that, whatever exploit we might undertake, we should consider ourselves as 'unprofitable servants' (Luke 17:10), because God, who is the Sole Existent, is also the Sole Agent.

The assertion that God is the sole architect and mason can be understood in two ways. First, it signifies that architecture is not properly speaking a human invention, but an art that God has 'taught' to man, just like agriculture: 'For his God doth instruct him (the ploughman) to discretion and doth teach him' (Isaiah 28:24–29). Architectural skill, in fact, is only the application of the physical and mathematical laws preexisting man in nature, which necessarily regulate both the arrangement of materials in a building and the general form of the latter, as we shall see. If he is to build, man can no more neglect these laws than he can the laws of vegetation if he is to cultivate the earth, or optics if he is to see. The human architect does nothing but rediscover or, in the Platonic sense, 'remember' these laws so as to submit to them. If it is the hands of man that move, it is essentially God who 'thinks' and 'builds'. Expressing the same idea, the Hindu Scriptures state that 'we should build as the gods did in the beginning.'[1] In the art of building, this reference to the Primordial Divine Activity is not foreign to Christian thought, as is shown by the following text: 'He is Infinite, we are finite; He constructs the world, we construct a house for Him.'[2] Besides, had not St Paul already written: 'For every house is built by some man; but He that built all things is God' (Heb. 3:4).[3]

But to say that God is the only architect can be understood in a yet more precise fashion in the case of the construction of the temple. Here, God is more directly the architect of His own abode. In

1. Cited by A.K. Coomaraswamy, *Christian and Oriental Philosophy of Art*, p73. Likewise Plotinus: 'The skills, like those of building and carpentry which give us fashioned objects ... draw their principles from there [the celestial world] and from celestial thought (*Enneads* v, 9).

2. Balai, *Prayer for the Dedication of a Church*, in G. Bickel, *Ausgew. Gedichte d. syr. Kirchenvater*, 77–82.

3. This text is used in the Russian ritual of dedication; see *Consécration d'une église selon le rituel de l'Église russe*, (Éd. Chevetogne), p14. The representation of the universe as a building site where God works after the manner of a master crafts-man inspired the meditation of an Egyptian sage: 'Man is clay and straw, God is the head of the site. Every day, he demolishes and builds. He does a thousand things according to his good pleasure; he makes a thousand people overseers' (*Sagesse*

fact, in traditional thought, the conception of the temple is the work of God himself. Otherwise put, the earthly temple is realized according to a heavenly archetype communicated to men through the intermediary of a prophet or other sacred figure. Thus the various sanctuaries of the Old Testament were built according to God's instructions. Everything regarding the Mosaic temple was the occasion for detailed prescriptions on the part of the Lord:

> And let them make me a sanctuary; that I may dwell among them. According to all that I show thee, after the pattern of the tabernacle, and the pattern of all the instruments thereof.... (Exod. 25:6–9).

David gave his son Solomon rules, received from God, that were to apply to the building of the new temple (1 Chron. 28:11–12). Ezekiel, in his turn, saw the description of the future temple in a vision: a supernatural being, with measuring stick in hand, gave the prophet both a general description and all the measurements of the building. (Ezek. 43:10–11).

Finally, the Heavenly Jerusalem, which descends from God, and the shape and dimensions of which were also taught St John by an angel, is the model of the Christian temple, as is amply proved by the layout of the latter, and affirmed by its ritual of consecration.[4] This belief in a celestial archetype of the temple has never disappeared in Christianity as is further shown by particular revelations, during the course of which God or the Blessed Virgin have communicated to saints not only their intention to see a sanctuary rise at a certain place, but precise indications as to its purpose and architectural layout. The remembrance of these facts has been perpetuated iconographically in scenes where we see the celestial figure presenting the

---

d'Amenemope [New Empire], cited in S. Morenz, *Relig. égypt.*, 1962, p99), and that of St Ignatius: 'God works and labors for me in all things created on the face of the earth—that is, behaves like one who labors—as in the heavens, elements, plants, fruits, cattle, etc., giving them being, preserving them, giving them vegetation and sensation...'(*Spiritual Exercises*, 'Contemplation to Gain Love', third point, Mullan translation).

4. We have developed these ideas in our book *The Symbolism of the Christian Temple*, pp 10, 17, 26.

earthly person with the 'model' of the temple to be constructed, or its plan. Thus, in a miniature of the Life of St Hugh (twelfth century), St Peter and St Paul appear in red to the abbot Gunzo, and mark out the plan of the future basilica of Cluny by laying out lines in front of him.[5]

However, the distinction we have made until now between an ordinary house and a temple is neither definitive nor absolute. If justified insofar as these two sorts of building are considered from the point of view of their peculiar characteristics, it becomes value-less when they are envisaged from a higher point of view, in their very nature as edifices.

The archetypal building is made up essentially of a base or floor, which provides the foundation for the dwelling, of a roof, which protects, and an intermediate space delimited and enclosed by walls. Now this archetypal building, by its very nature, reproduces the architecture of the universe in such a way that its base corresponds to the earth, its intermediate space to the air, and its roof to the heavenly vault.[6]

From this it follows that the house is a symbol of the universe, which, in a way, is the primordial House of Man; and, as a result, the building of a house will also reproduce or imitate the creation of the world. Or again, creation can legitimately be conceived as a building. Moreover, this is the point of view alluded to by the Hindu text cited above: 'We should build as the gods did in the beginning.'

In this perspective, God is the Architect of the universe; and because of this He is the architect of the house, for architecture would not exist if there were not an architecture of the world; the latter is the sufficient and necessary reason for the former.

The theme of God as the architect of the universe is to be found in both the Pythagorean and Platonic traditions of the Greeks, and in the Bible. For Plato, God is the Surveyor who constructs the

---

5. L. Spink, *L'art sacré en Occident et en Orient*, 1962, pl. 1.

6. Coomaraswamy, op. cit., pp79–80. The Platonic theme passed to Plutarch, where God appeared as the architect of the world, constructing it according to numbers and proportions (Plut., *De anim. Procr.*, at the end).

world according to the principles symbolized by the five regular polyhedrons, the expressions of formal perfection. Nicomachus of Gerasa, a commentator of Plato, said of the number Ten that it 'serves as the measure of the universe, as a square and line in the hand of the Director.'[7]

From the Platonists, the idea passed to the scholars and artists of the Middle-Ages. In the miniatures of this period, God is shown with a compass in hand tracing a circle on the original chaos, shown as the mouth of a dragon.[8] On a pillar in *Notre Dame de Paris* we can see an iron plaque placed by the Company of Masons, which bears the inscription 'To the Glory of the Great Architect of the Universe' engraved above a pentagon, a ruler, a pair of compasses, and a square.[9]

This representation has scriptural foundations, the most explicit of which is this magnificent passage from Job (3:4–6), in which God says to man,

Where wast thou when I laid the *foundations* of the earth? . . . Who hath laid the *measures* thereof. . . ? Or who hath stretched the *line* upon it? Whereupon are the *columns* thereof fixed? Or who laid the *cornerstone* thereof?

The symbolism will be complete if we add this invocation from a liturgical text: 'O Thou, the divine *Framer* of the heavenly vault.'[10]

The text from Job evokes the splendor of the original world, spoilt by sin. But God decided to rebuild it. And this new world in the making is the Church, both the earthly and heavenly. The Church is the Holy City, 'the masterpiece' of the divine Artisan. 'It is God who builds Jerusalem' (Psalm 46). Scripture teaches us that God is the

---

7. Nicomachus of Gerasa, *Theologoumena*, cited in M. Ghyka, *Le Nombre d'or*, I, p36.

8. E.g. in the thirteenth century *Bible moralisée* of Vienna (Codex Vindobonensis 2554 der Österreichischen Nationalbibliothek), and in a fourteenth-century Bible reproduced in J. Gimpel, *Les batisseurs des cathedrales*, p32.

9. S. Hutin, *L'Alchimie*, p94.

10. *Consecr. d'une eglise...russe*, p36.

master of works of the spiritual city: 'By faith he (Abraham) sojourned in the land of promise, as in a strange country ... for he looked for a city which hath eternal foundations, whose *architect and mason* is God' (Heb. 11:9–10). It is Christ who came to found this city on earth, and He too presented himself as Architect when He said to Simon: 'Thou art Peter and upon this rock *I will build my church*' (Matt. 16:18).

As the Church of stone is the symbol of the Spiritual Church, the whole liturgy for setting the first stone and for the Dedication develop the themes of construction related to the image of the heavenly Jerusalem, and included at every step is the theme of the divine Architect. This goes back to the very earliest days of Christianity. Eusebius relates how St Paulinus built the great basilica of Tyre, telling us that the Word Himself, the great Ordainer of all things, Himself became a copy on earth of the Heavenly Archetype which is the Church of the first-born in heaven, the Jerusalem On-High, the Mountain of God and the City of the living God.[11]

This dimension of symbolism should not make us forget another, that of the relationship between temple and cosmos, for it also belongs to the same spiritual perspective. The building of a temple is compared in the liturgy to the work of Creation. Thus, in the Coptic rite, the readings of the long vigil preceding the consecration begin with the Genesis account of Creation, and end with the vision of the heavenly Jerusalem from the Apocalypse, while the intermediate readings recall the erection of the baetyl of Jacob and the divine prescriptions relating to the different temples mentioned above. The purpose of this sequence of sacred readings, at this juncture, is to make us understand that the construction of a church is a gift of God inserted into the whole Economy of salvation and that of the world.[12] A magnificent text of the Byzantine-Slavic rite of dedication says, in the same sense,

> You, Lord, the Divine Framer of the heavenly vault and Builder of the church ... by a command you have erected the earth upon

---

11. Eusebius, *Hist. eccl.*, x, 65.
12. R. Coquin, *La consécration d'une église selon le rite copte*. In *Os*, 9, 1954, p 173.

the abyss. . . . Steady your church on the unshakable rock of your commandments, O Christ, the only good one and lover of mankind.[13]

The Roman ritual for the placing of the first stone of a church—one faithful, moreover, to all the traditional rituals—stipulates that the officiant acts in the place of God. In pursuance of this, the ritual uses the text from Isaiah 28:16, repeated by St Peter: 'Behold, I lay in Sion a chief corner stone, elect, precious: and he that believeth on him shall not be confounded' (1 Pet. 2:6). St Paul, for his part, teaches us that 'Jesus Christ himself [is] the chief cornerstone; in whom all the building fitly framed together groweth into an holy temple in the Lord: in whom ye also are builded together. . . .' (Eph. 2:20–22). And the same ritual includes a prayer that restores to Christ the task of building:

Lord Jesus Christ, who art the cornerstone taken from the mountain without human aid, secure this stone that should be placed in Your Name. Thou art the Beginning and the End, it is through this Cause that God the Father created everything at the beginning; mayest Thou, we pray Thee, be the cause, the development and the completion of this work. . . .[14]

The stone taken from the mountain is an image of the Messiah that comes from the Old Testament (Dan. 2:34–35). It appears again in a hymn from the Feast of the Dedication according to the Roman rite, which sings of Christ the cornerstone reuniting the two cities:

From the heights of Heaven
The Son of the sovereign Father,
Stone hewn from the mountain
And falling to earth,
Has reunited through the angels
The dwelling above and that here below.[15]

---

13. *Consecr. d'une église...russe*, p36.
14. Dubois, *Cérémonial de la pose de la première pierre d'une église*, 1927, pp16 and 6.
15. Hymn of Lauds (Common of a Dedication).

The construction of the church of stone is obviously a symbol of the construction of the Spiritual Church, of the growth of the Mystical Body, of the total Christ. This growth was already defined in architectural terms by St Paul in the text cited above (see also Col. 2:7 and Eph. 4:7–13). One of the first works of Christian literature, *The Shepherd*, written by Hermas in the second century, portrays the development of the Church under the allegory of a great tower built of stones that are the saints, that is, the baptized.[16] This image of living stones is a revealed image from the First Epistle of St Peter:

> To whom coming, as to a living stone, rejected indeed by men, but chosen and made honorable by God, be you also living stones built up, a spiritual house. . . . (1:4–5).

In truth, however, it is not we ourselves who form the building, but Christ, at once the object and subject of the construction, the Living Stone and Architect. It is He who arranges us, also living stones, in order to bring us into the Temple of the Church. This is the meaning of another prayer of the ritual:

> God, who from all the assembled saints raises a temple to Thine eternal Majesty, add new stones to this spiritual edifice so that, founded by Thy command, it will be completed through the power of Thy Goodness.[17]

The figure of the Divine Artisan is, however, more precisely developed in a liturgical hymn to the glory of the Heavenly Temple, the Jerusalem On-High. Here, too, the Architect is the dresser of stones, who transforms us from rough stones into cubic stones capable of occupying a place in the building:

> Celestial City of Jerusalem,
> Blessed vision of peace,
> Who, built of living stones,
> Rises even to the stars,
> And, like a bride, is surrounded
> By thousands upon thousands of angels. . . .

16. Hermas, *The Shepherd*, 1, vision 3.
17. Dubois, op. cit., p16.

Under the blows of the wholesome chisel,
Repeatedly struck by the Workman's hammer,
The stones are dressed to form this edifice:
Fitly joined, to the zenith they rise.[18]

In his *Treatise on the Psalms* and his *Sermons*, St Augustine developed at length the themes condensed in the last verse of this hymn. It is through the intermediary of His ministers, he says, that Christ dresses the living stones:

The stones are extracted from the mountain by the preachers of the truth, and are squared so as to be able to form part of the eternal edifice. There are presently many stones in the hands of the Workman. May Heaven grant that they fall not from His hands, so that, once their dressing is completed, they may be integrated into the construction of the temple, that is to say of Jerusalem 'built like a city', whose foundation is Christ Himself.[19]

Elsewhere he proposes an allegorical exegesis of the different movements of the mason who quarries and polishes the stone. The spiritual edifice, he says, rises when believers are united in Christ: 'Their act of faith is, in a way, like the quarrying of the stone. Together, their catechesis, baptism, and formation are the squaring, sizing and leveling.' And the cement that bonds the stones, making of them the fitly joined stones of the hymn, is the cement of Love: 'The believers only become the House of the Lord if they are united by Love.'[20]

The outlines of a complete architectural conception of the Christian story can be seen running through all these Scriptural, liturgical, and patristic texts.

---

18. Hymn of Vespers (Common of a Dedication). The allegorical meaning of the cubic form of stones goes back to an ancient tradition: see our book cited above, pp 65–66.

19. St Augustine, *In Psalm.* 121 (lesson second day within the octave of the dedication of a church, at the second nocturne).

20. St Augustine, *Serm.* 256 *de tempore* (lesson third day within the octave of the dedication of a church, at the second nocturne).

The unfolding of this story appears as the spiritual construction of a new world, the New Jerusalem, which, under the direction of the Great Architect, is the work of all. It unfolds in three phases. In the first, Christ comes to earth to lay the first or foundation stone, which ultimately is none other than Himself. In the second phase, upon this foundation, of which Simon Peter is the visible substitute, the Temple is built with living stones, which are the believers. Finally, in the third phase, the building is completed with the placing of the keystone of the vault, which is again Christ, the Beginning and End, Alpha and Omega.[21] Then the whole building undergoes a glorious transmutation, the stones becoming precious and shining in the Divine Light. At this point, the Heavenly City appears in all its splendor, which tore these passionate words from Epiphanius of Salamis:

O paradise of the Grand Architect, City of the Holy King, Betrothed of Christ, immaculate, Virgin all-pure, promised in the Faith to the unique Bridegroom, you radiate and shine like the dawn![22]

---

21. On the various, apparently contradictory meanings of the expression 'cornerstone', see the definitive explanations of R. Guénon (articles reprinted in *Symbols of Sacred Science*, p264 ff.) and the consequences we have drawn from them in our book, p114 ff. On the same subject also read the beautiful chapter devoted to 'L'Église et les temples d'Israël' in J. Tourniac, *Symbolisme maçonnique et Tradition chrétienne*, 1965, pp166–177.

22. *Hymn to the Church* in *The Panarion*, 3, *Exposition of the Faith* (PG 42, 776).

LAON CATHEDRAL

'The book of all the secrets of creation, the Living Book that the divine Scribe, who has 'the words of eternal life', never ceases writing.' [page 13] ➤

'The spider can, with reason, even be chosen as a symbol of the divinity, in that it fashions its web from its own substance, just as God creates the world ... from the Ideas and according to the archetype contained in His Mind.' [page 43]

AMIENS CATHEDRAL

'The construction of the church of stone is obviously a symbol of the construction of the Spiritual Church, of the growth of the Mystical Body, of the total Christ.' [page 52]

AMIENS CATHEDRAL

'Here [Christ] appears in the guise of a warrior of gigantic proportions, a cosmic warrior engaged in a universal battle.' [page 27]

AMIENS CATHEDRAL

'Here ... the Architect is the dresser of stones, who transforms us from rough stones into cubic stones capable of occupying a place in the building.... And the cement that bonds the stones, making of them the fitly joined stones of the hymn, is the cement of Love.' [pages 52–53]

LAON CATHEDRAL

'The ultimate end of every creature...is to "gather what is scattered". That is to say, by means of the spiritual way to leave multiplicity in order to re-enter Unity; to quit manifestation in order to return to its Principle; to abandon Time for Eternity.' [pages 67–68]

LAON CATHEDRAL

'At its own level, the gesture of molding reproduces in a particularly striking way the process of creation, which is defined ontologically as the descent of form into matter, the imprinting of the essence upon substance.' [page 35]

The myste
the secret
crafts,
arou

The th

Creation,
divine
ayed
egg of
rld.

rlds

AMIENS CATHEDRAL

'the spiritual construction of a new world, the New Jerusalem, which, under the direction of the Great Architect, is the work of all.' [page 54]

LAON CATHEDRAL

'The scriptural comparison of man to a tree planted in the Garden of God, starting with the Man-God assimilated to the Tree of Life....' [page 82]

◄—
LAON CATHEDRAL (overleaf)

'All occupations imitate God, Who is ceaselessly at work, for He ceaselessly creates the world.' [page 4]

AMIENS CATHEDRAL

'...the world in its turn can be seen as a garden, with God the Creator as the Gardener who conceived, designed, realized, and planted it at the beginning, and whose Providence continues to care for it throughout the course of time.' [page 76]

LAON CATHEDRAL

Meister Eckhart: 'God has cast His net and lasso over all creatures, in such a way that it can be discovered and recognized in each of them.' [pages 73–74]

AMIENS CATHEDRAL

'He has Himself become the seed and ear, and the gift He offers is Himself as food.' [pages 93–94]

CHURCH OF ST. NICHOLAS OF HAGUENAU

'Christ the mystical grape cluster, crushed by the heavenly Vine-grower in the Passion, gives us His Blood, and the Wine He offers us… is truly the drink of immortality.' [page 99]

7

The
'Son of
the Carpenter'

IN THE GOSPEL, Jesus is called 'the son of the carpenter [Joseph]' (Matt. 13:55) and 'the carpenter' (Mark 6:3).[1] This designation should be given full consideration, for it is of the utmost importance. Doubtless it can be very simply explained by the context in which it is found, for the words are those of the people of Nazareth who murmured against Jesus, who had come to speak in the synagogue of his native town. 'Is this not the son of the carpenter?' they said. But every word of Scripture, beyond its obvious sense, conceals a deeper one, for, being the word of God, it necessarily has a

---

1. There has been some debate about the meaning of the Greek word *tekton*, and some prefer to follow the Vulgate in translating it simply as *faber*, 'artisan'. However, there is hardly any doubt as to the meaning of *tekton*, as of *naggar*, which corresponds to it in Aramaic. The primary meaning of *tekton* is 'carpenter', 'joiner'. Sometimes, it is true, it has the sense of 'artisan', general 'worker', but this meaning is hardly encountered except in poetry. The usual Greek words to express 'artisan' or 'worker' are *ergates*, *chironax*, and *technites dimiourgos*. Moreover, in the tradition concerning the childhood of Christ, it is the sense of 'carpenter' that prevails. Although Justin made St Joseph a maker of yokes and ploughs (*Dialogus cum tryphone*), Jesus' adoptive father was very much a true carpenter, for Theophilus of Antioch (*In Matthaeum*, 13), as also for the author of the *Opus imperfectum* (*Auctor. oper. Imperfectum in Matthaeum homil.* 1), and for the apocryphal writings: *Protevangelium of James*, 6 and 13: *Pseudo-Matthew*, 10 and 42 (where Joseph teaches Jesus carpentry) and the *Story of Joseph the Carpenter*. — The traditional presumption that makes carpenters of both Joseph and Jesus suffices as a point of departure for us. What we shall say in due course will considerably strengthen this hypothesis, even though this will not be by way of the famous 'higher criticism'.

universal bearing. What is more, anyone slightly familiar with the modes of expression of Sacred Scripture knows well that at times an important teaching can easily find support on an apparently precarious footing. Besides, if even in the life of an ordinary person nothing happens by chance, then even more so must everything in the life of Christ have a profound reason for being manifested. If, then, Jesus chose during his hidden life to practice the trade of carpentry in Joseph's workshop, this will of necessity have a meaning. The occupation of carpenter, so close to those of architect and mason just studied, also expresses in its own way the function and mission of Christ as the Creative Word and Redeemer.

Once again, this symbolism belongs to the universal domain of the sacred. Just as there are architect gods, so there are carpenter gods. In both cases it is a question of creator gods, the cosmogonic process being assimilated to the art of construction, which appeals as much to the techniques of stone as it does to those of wood. The techniques of wood, inseparable from architecture, are also used in other skills such as shipbuilding, furniture making, and statuary.

In Nordic mythology, God, in order to create man, animated a matter called *trê*, a word signifying 'tree' or 'wood'.[2] Likewise in India. According to the Vedas, the world was created from wood by the Divine Carpenter,[3] who is sometimes Tvashtri and at others Vishvakarman; he also had various functional names, such as 'universal artisan',[4] 'fashioner of things', 'he who molds forms',[5] 'celestial architect',[6] and more especially 'carpenter'. As such, it is he who assembles and fits together the different pieces of the cosmos;[7] he is shown in the midst of his workers and when he is united to his *shakti*

---

2. Grimm, *Teutonic Mythology*, vol. 2, tr. from fourth ed. (New York: Dover Publications, 1966), p571.

3. *Rig-Veda*, x, 31, 7; 81, 4; 89, 7.

4. J. Herbert, *Message de la mythologie hindoue*, p84.

5. Ibid., p314

6. Ibid., p56.

7. Ibid., p314.

or creative energy, 'the entire world is assembled' like the pieces of a framework, which, from simple beams, become a house.[8]

At a less elevated level, the divine hero or prophet whose mission it is not to create, but to renew the world, is often also the son of a carpenter or himself a carpenter. Thus, according to a legend found among the Arabs, but of Jewish origin,[9] Terah, the father of Abraham, who was the heir to traditional orthodoxy and the founder of the People of Israel, was an artisan skilled in the carving of pegs and divine images. He was therefore a joiner and sculptor. Noah, the founder of a regenerated world after the catastrophe of the flood, was the carpenter who made the ark; we shall return to this. The father of Tammuz—better known as Adonis—the divine hero of the Phoenicians, was Kinyras, a carpenter who was said to have invented the hammer, the lever, and roofing. Adonis himself is called both 'son of the carpenter' or 'carpenter'.[10]

The case of Adonis, which is very interesting, calls for some clarification. A parallel is often drawn between the myth of Adonis and the story of Jesus, and, in a certain sense, there are no grounds for challenging it. However, let it be well understood that this is certainly not to adopt a rationalist point of view which seeks to explain the 'myth' of Jesus by means of the relics of other earlier myths. Such a point of view is not only inadmissible for a Christian, but also unacceptable to anyone who has a sense of the true science of religions. This being said, it should be remembered that in Christianity there are the dogmas, on the one hand, and on the other, their formulation. The formulation is necessarily accomplished in the Holy Scriptures by images and symbols. And these latter are not just any image or symbol; they are *sacred* symbols and images which can, and even, in a certain way, must be the same in Christianity and other religions, given that here it is a question of universal and fundamental images belonging to the primordial orthodox Revelation,

---

8. Ibid., p84.

9. In the *Shalshelet ha-kabbala* cited by Migne, *Dict. Bible*, s.v. Thare.

10. Ch. Autran, *Préhistoire de Christianisme*, i, pp174–75. Adonis is also called 'born of the cedar'. This second epithet perhaps expresses the idea that he was the carpenter par excellence.

whatever might sometimes be its deformations. Thus, it was the opinion of our earliest Fathers that, in God's plan, certain heroes, even pagans, were well able to prefigure Our Lord Jesus Christ. Nothing therefore prevents us from considering the legend of Adonis, 'son of the carpenter', from this angle.[11]

Thus the artisanal calling inherited from Joseph and exercised by Jesus expresses in its own way the meaning of Christ's divine activity and earthly function.

Jesus is the 'son of the carpenter' Joseph, who, as the earthly father of Christ, is a reflection of the divine Carpenter, the heavenly Father. But Jesus is Himself a carpenter and under this aspect is shown as the creator of the world and as its renovator through His Church.

The material the carpenter works with is wood. Jesus, the cosmic Carpenter, as the creative Word, works the Wood, which is to say Prime Matter, from which the entire world comes forth. It is remarkable, in fact, that in numerous traditions the word designating *wood* serves equally to designate *matter* in general: in Greek, *hyle*, in Latin *materies* (whence the French *matière* and the Spanish *madera*, 'wood'), and in Hebrew *e'tz*, while in Egyptian *khet* expresses both the idea of wood and that of object, 'thing'.[12] In the same way the tree, which gives its wood, is a well-known image of the world. In every tradition there exists a cosmic Tree, symbolizing the whole of Creation considered as a living organism and structured according to the two axes, the vertical and the horizontal, embodied in the trunk and the branches. The shape of the tree is not other than the Cross.

The wood that Jesus the carpenter works is the wood of the

---

11. This brings to mind the famous passage from St Jerome. 'Bethlehem, which belongs to us now and is the most august place in the universe, of which the Psalmist said: "The Truth has come forth from the earth," was in times gone by shaded by a tree sacred to Tammuz, or Adonis. And in the grotto, where one day the Christ child cried, they wept for the lover of Venus' (*Letters of St. Paulinus of Nola*, PL 61, 326–27). Furthermore, Hiram, the architect of the temple, also came from Phoenicia.

12. A. Ermanm, H. Grapow, *Wörterbuch der aegyptischen Sprache*, III, 341.

Cross. The cross is the essential figure of all carpentry work and of all architecture, in that it expresses the co-ordinates of space.[13] The wood of the cross is the cosmic tree[14] from which the Divine Carpenter makes the world, and the tree of the cross as such is the spiritual blueprint according to which Jesus the Carpenter reconstructs the world, or builds the new world.

This new world is the Church, often compared to a ship the biblical 'type' of which is the Ark, the work of the carpenter Noah. Now Noah is a figure of Christ, as the Ark is a figure of the Church. This is a widely developed theme in Patristic literature. According to Origen, 'Our Lord is our Noah, whom the Father at the end of time has ordered to make an ark.'[15] Moreover, he relates the three dimensions of the Ark—the length, the breadth, and the height—to those of the Cross suggested by the famous passage from the Epistle to the Ephesians (3:18).

Sometimes the cross is the mast of the Church as ship, as in this hymn of Lent: 'Jesus Savior, our ship, whose mast is the Cross, has already crossed the greater part of the course of fasts....' (Triodion, Monday of the fourth week of Lent). At other times, in conformity with Origen's interpretation and by way of a metonymy analogous to that of classical authors and full of meaning, the Ark itself is assimilated to the Tree of the Cross. 'Having to cross the waves of the stormy sea of time, we climb confidently onto the Wood of the Cross and spread the sails of our faith before the favorable wind of the Holy Spirit'; 'Without sinking, the Church crosses the sea of time upon the Wood of Thy Cross.'[16] 'Lofty Tree.., marked with the precious blood that flowed from the body of the Lamb, you are the Ark for this shipwrecked world, taking it back to port,' (Hymn of Good Friday, *Pange lingua*).

Conversely, the Ark is called Wood, *lignum*; like the Cross, it is the *lignum vitae* or *arbor vitae*. Scripture says of it, *Benedictum est*

13. We develop these ideas in our book, *The Symbolism of the Christian Temple*.

14. On the cosmic tree, see M. Eliade, *Patterns in Comparative Religion*; H. Rahner, *Greek Myths and Christian Mysteries*, and our book cited above.

15. *In Genesim Homiliae* ii, 3.

16. Hymns from the Gothic missals of Spain cited in AL, *Le temps pascal* i, p340; ii, p82.

lignum per quod fit justitia (Wisd. 10:4; 14:7), 'Blessed the Wood that has produced Justice,' for it condemns the world, saves the righteous Noah, and announces the redemptive Cross.

The Ark is a product of the art of carpentry and is thereby linked to the 'occupation' of Jesus. But we have seen that the building of the Church also depends upon the art of masonry, the perspective within which Jesus appeared as architect and mason: 'Upon this rock I shall build my Church....' Now in this latter perspective, Jesus does not cease to play His role as carpenter. In the previous chapter we said that from the point of view of masonry, the history of the Church can in fact be reduced to a construction in three phases: the placing of the first stone, the building of the walls, and the placing of the key stone. By adding the point of view of carpentry, we can envisage a fourth phase: the covering of the building with the roof. Here again, it is the 'son of the carpenter' who intervenes to finish the construction at the end of the ages and return the work to His Father.

It is important to define this parallel more closely. The role played in masonry by the corner or keystone which, in uniting the arch supports, and thereby enabling the whole structure to 'hold together', is analogous to that of the vertical beam or king post, indispensable to the assembly of the elements of the roof trusses. Moreover, both the one and the other are situated on the vertical axis which orders the whole building in its vertical dimension, and is symbolically identical with the world Axis and the vertical beam of the Cross, which are one.[17]

Now, to this analogy between the functions there corresponds a striking parallel between what Scripture says about the keystone and what the mediaeval legend of the Wood of Life says about the beam of the cross. According to this legend, the wood of the cross came from the seed of the Tree of Life in Eden, handed down by

---

17. We have explored this question in our study cited above. The Greek word for cross, *stavros*, means 'pillar'; it refers to the vertical beam that the first Fathers assimilated to the Cosmic Pillar or Axis of the World (see H. Rahner).

Seth. The story relates that from the tree that grew from that seed a beam was made, which 'Solomon placed at the site of the Temple.' But a master carpenter said *the wood was good for nothing and threw it into a hole full of mud.* Nevertheless, the beam was rescued and buried in the vicinity of the Pool of Bethesda, where it was discovered at the moment of the Passion and made into the Cross of Christ.[18] The parallel with the keystone, the stone that was first 'rejected by the builders,' but which 'became the head of the corner' (Matt. 21:42), is immediately evident. In the Gospel passage, Jesus compares himself to the Keystone, the crown of the edifice, the highest point of the axial pillar, and 'gate of heaven'. Analogously, is the master beam of the Cross not also Christ?

We are faced here with a frequently occurring sacred schema, in which the subject and object are interchangeable. Christ is both architect and mason of the world and the Church, but He is also the corner stone, just as, in the sacrifice, He is both priest and victim. Here, He is both carpenter and king post of the roof-truss, that post or beam which is none other than the Tree of Life. According to Honorius of Autun, 'The Tree of Life is Wisdom, the Life of Souls; this tree, this wood, is Christ. . . . Or rather it is the Cross that bears Christ. Christ is justifiably compared to a tree.'[19]

Thus, through His death upon the Cross, Christ-the-Carpenter purifies the Wood, that is to say, universal Substance, with His blood, and breathes anew the principle of life into it. 'Water and blood flow together from His wound, and the earth, the ocean, the stars, and the world are washed by this divine stream' (*Hymn Pange Lingua*). Then, as the axis of the new world and mast of the Ark of the Church, He raises towards heaven the beam of the Tree of Life which, like Jacob's ladder, reunites earth to heaven. In this way, the 'son of the carpenter', who is also the 'son of David' and 'son of the King' completely fulfils the words of the Prophet: *Regnabit a ligno Deus*, 'God will reign through the Wood.'

18. This legend appears in Gossuin, *Image du monde*, the *Bible de Geffroi de Paris*, the *Historia ecclesiastica* of Petrus Cosmestor (PL 198) and the *Queste del Saint Graal.*

19. *Expos. in psalm. Select.* I, 3 (PL 172, 277) and *In Annuntiat. Sanct. Mariae* (PL 172, 902).

8

Pastor et Nauta

IN THE 'prophecy of the Popes', said to be 'from Malachy', the device attributed to His Holiness John XXXIII is *Pastor et nauta*, that is, 'Shepherd and pilot'. We have absolutely no intention of discussing here the value that should be accorded this 'prophecy';[1] we simply think that, taken in itself, the formula *Pastor et nauta* suits the Pope perfectly, whoever he might be. It sums up two pontifical functions that reflect here below two divine functions or 'occupations', which are, moreover, very closely related to each other. Together they manifest the power of God, not as Creator, but rather as Providence, in the government of the Church and the world.

The theme of the Good Shepherd is well known. Nevertheless, if we are to understand the full depth of this symbolism and at the same time its parallels with that of the pilot, it will be worth recalling the principal texts mapping its development in Scripture, from the Old Testament to Jesus.

In the Psalms, the Lord is the 'Shepherd of Israel': 'Give ear, O Shepherd of Israel, thou that leadest Joseph like a flock' (Psalm 79). Psalm 22 is a wonderful sacred pastoral poem; in it, the inspired author expresses, in words full of sweetness, the perfect confidence and joy of the believer: 'The Lord is my shepherd, I shall not want. He maketh me to lie down in green pastures. . . .' The theme is

---

1. On this subject, see the evocative pages of J. Tourniac, *Symbolisme maçonnique et tradition chrétienne*, p 131 ff.

amplified in the prophets: Isaiah (39:11), Jeremiah (31:11), Ezekiel (34:23), Micah (7:14), Zechariah (11:4): 'He that scattered Israel will gather him, and keep him, as a shepherd doth his flock,' says Jeremiah. And in a long chapter, Ezekiel develops and brings together nearly all the elements of this theme that are to be found in the Gospels. The pastor gathers the lost sheep, leads them on paths, pastures them on the mountains of the Eternal, on green pastures near running brooks, and finally searches for the injured sheep and takes care of it. This is already the self-portrait that Christ was pleased to leave us:

> I am the door of the sheep. . . . I am the door: by me if any man enter in, he shall be saved, and shall go in and out, and find pasture. . . . I am come that they might have life, and that they might have it more abundantly. . . . I am the good shepherd: the good shepherd giveth his life for the sheep. . . . I know my sheep, and am known of mine. . . . I lay down my life for the sheep. And other sheep I have, which are not of this fold: them also I must bring, and they shall hear my voice; and there shall be one fold and one shepherd (John 10:7–16).

Compare the parable of the lost sheep (Luke 15), and the scene of the sheep and the goats at the Last Judgment (Matt. 25).

When Jesus left this world, it was Peter, his 'vicar', who was to be the good shepherd. That is why one of the enthronement rites of Peter as Head of the Church took the form of a conferment of the title of shepherd. Three times Jesus asked him: 'Peter, lovest thou me?' and with each of the Apostle's affirmative responses, said to him, 'Feed my lambs . . . feed my sheep' (John 21:15–17).[2]

Later, Peter would in turn say to the other bishops and to the priests, 'Feed the flock confided to you. . . . And when the Prince of Shepherds shall appear, you will receive the incorruptible crown of glory' (1 Pet. 5:2–4 and 1 Pet. 2:25).

It is hardly surprising that among a nomadic people like the Jews—at least in their origins—the station of shepherd should be

---

2. The other enthronement of Peter consisted in the bestowing of his new name (*Cephas* = Rock) and the conferring of the power of the keys.

held in such high esteem. Moreover, the soul of the shepherd, who is always a semi-nomad, is open to contemplation and, in principle, he is closer to God than the sedentary and the townsman, being less attached to this world. In this regard, we note that Abel, the righteous, was a shepherd, whereas Cain was a farmer, and that it was to the shepherds that the Nativity was first announced.

In the New Testament, nautical symbolism is as important as pastoral. It develops in three directions: that of walking on water (John 6:14–21; Matt. 14:24–33), that of fishing, and that of voyaging. Only the last theme will be dealt with here.

The fishing boat that Jesus boards with His disciples forms part of the Gospel 'landscape', of which it is one of the principal components. Without doubt, the most important passage is that of the stilling of the storm:

> And when he was entered into a ship, his disciples followed him. And, behold, there arose a great tempest in the sea, insomuch that the ship was covered with the waves: but he was asleep. And his disciples came to him, and awoke him, saying, Lord, save us: we perish. And he saith unto them, Why are ye fearful, O ye of little faith? Then he arose, and rebuked the wind and the seas; and there was a great calm (Matt. 8:23–27).

Commenting on this text, St Augustine extracts its spiritual meaning. 'The ship,' he says, 'is the Church; the wild sea, the world where we live.'[3] But the exegesis is older, and comes from Hippolytus of Rome, who is more precise: 'The sea is the world; the Church, like a ship, is battered by the waves, but not submerged. She has, in fact, an experienced pilot, Christ.'[4]

We see here emerging the theme of God the pilot. In the Gospel account, however, it is not Christ, but Peter and the disciples, who

---

3. St Augustine, *De verbo Domini*.

4. Hyppolytus of Rome, *Treatise on Christ and Antichrist*, 59;. *Apostolic Constitution* II, 57. On these texts, see J. Daniélou, *Primitive Christian Symbols*, tr. D. Attwater (Baltimore: Helicon Press, 1964), p 58 ff.

steer the boat while Jesus sleeps. There is nothing contradictory in this, however; Peter is indeed the visible pilot of the Church, but is so 'in the Name of God', and it is ultimately Christ who leads the Church, but invisibly; Jesus sleeping in the ship symbolizes that 'non-acting activity' that belongs to God.

The barque of Peter, the ship of the Church, has an illustrious antecedent in Scripture: the ark of Noah. There are innumerable comparisons in the tradition of the Fathers between these two ships on the one hand, and between the Gospel's raging sea (= the world) and the destroying flood on the other. 'The Ark of Noah was the prefiguration of the Church,' says St Jerome.[5] In fact, the Church is indeed the *arca salutis*, the Ark of salvation; the Preface of the Mass of Dedication takes over this idea, applying it to both the temple of stone and the spiritual Church. 'It is the Ark that saves us from the flood of this world and brings us to the port of salvation.'[6] Within the same perspective, a parallel has sometimes been drawn between Christ and Noah. Christ, according to Origen, is 'the Noah designated by the Father to make the Ark from squared timber and give it proportions full of heavenly mysteries.'[7]

Why should it surprise us if the images of the shepherd and pilot have been universally adopted as emblems of the king or the chief, to the very extent that the latter are 'God's lieutenants' on earth? Homer, Pindar, the authors of the Tragedies, and Plato, call the king 'the shepherd of peoples'. Isaiah himself said that Cyrus was 'the shepherd of the Eternal'(44:28). As for the word 'govern', which we use to designate the administration of society, it comes from the Latin *guberno* (Greek: *kyberno*) which, in the first place, expresses the piloting of a ship. In Greek, the pilot is called: *kybernetes*. 'He who pilots a ship,' says Iamblicus, 'represents the power that governs

5. St Jerome, PL23, 185A. On this whole theme, see J. Danielou, *Sacramentum futuri*, pp69–85.
6. On the ship of salvation and posthumous navigation, an Egyptian idea that passed to Crete and from there to the Greco-Roman world, see F. Cumont, *Lux perpetua*, pp283–286.
7. Origen, *In Genesim Homiliae*, II, 3.

the world, that is to say, the divine Sun.'[8] The same image is to be found in the Iliad where Zeus appears as the 'supreme pilot', *hypsyzygos.*[9] It will be understood, then, why royal initiation in Greece included a crossing of water by swimming, and on a ship,[10] and also a guarding of flocks. Philo was following exactly the same line of thought when, writing the *Life of Moses*, he observed, 'The care needed in guarding flocks is a preparation for kingship.'[11] These symbols are transparent, obvious, so to speak, on the human and social plane. They do not have any less value and meaning on the divine plane. Again, Philo has left us a magnificent exposition on God, the supreme shepherd of the universe:

The task of the shepherd is so important that it is rightly attributed not only to kings, sages, and souls of perfect purity, but even to the sovereign God. . . . Like a flock, the earth, the water, the air, the fire, all the plants also, all the beings found there, both mortal and divine, the nature of heaven too, the revolutions of the sun and the moon, and more, the variations and harmonious movements of all the stars, are all led by God, shepherd and king, according to Justice and the Law. . . .[12]

Commenting on the initiatic swim, Porphyry says that it represents the passage across the impure waters of the world to reach the firm shore where the glory of God shines.[13] The spiritual meaning of the sea voyage is perfectly defined by Simplicius, another of the ancients:

---

8. Iamblicus, *De mysteriis,* 7, 2. The same image occurs in Plato where God is 'the pilot of the universe' (*The Statesman* 272E [and from 269C]). In Egypt, too, the world was a ship and the Universal Master its pilot, as can be seen in *l'Enseignement d'Amenope* (J. Vandier, *La religion égyptienne,* pp225–6).

9. *Iliad* 7, 69; 4, 166. The image passed into Orphism: 'Zeus is the master-pilot of the universe' (*Orph. Frag.* VI, 10). Cf. Morenz, *Relig. egypt.,* 1962, 95 (references).

10. At Eleusis, for example. See V. Magnien, *Les mystères d'Éleusis,* pp325 and 333–6.

11. Philo, *De vita Moysis* 1, 11. This was said apropos the flocks of Jethro. On the mystical sense of these flocks, see J. Daniélou, *Sacramentum Futuri,* p180.

12. Philo, *De agricultura,* 50–51 and 41.

13. Porphyry, *Vita Plotini* in Plotin, ed. Bréhier, I, p25.

The sea was said to be the symbol of becoming; the vessel will be what transports souls in the world of becoming, that is to say, of fate and destiny.... The pilot of the ship will be God who directs and governs the All....[14]

Moreover, it is known that the mythical voyages, like the circumnavigation of Ulysses and the expedition of the Argonauts, have a mystical meaning.[15]

It will now be seen how these two symbols clarify each other. The shepherd is the one who nourishes, guards, and guides the sheep through dangers; likewise, the pilot on his ship shelters the voyagers and conducts them through the perils of the waves (= men through the dangers of life). But this is still not the essential. Looking more closely, we see that the shepherd *gathers* his sheep and leads them back to the sheepfold, where they are reunited (cf. the text of Ezekiel above). In like manner, the perishing voyagers, scattered over the waves, are *gathered* into the ship by the pilot and guided to port, the goal of the journey and place of security after all the perils. In its most obvious spiritual sense, this means that merciful Providence seeks to guide us during the course of this life towards the 'fold' or the 'port', which are also 'salvation'. Just as Noah *gathered* the living into the Ark so as to *save* them, so Christ gathers us into His Church, the vessel that cannot but reach the eternal shore. Thus, according to Dante, the function of the Roman Pontiff, of Peter in his barque, is to guide humanity to port 'after the waves of insinuating greed have been stilled.' In their highest meaning, which corresponds with this saying of Jesus, 'Whoever gathers not with me, scatters,' these two symbols designate the ultimate end of every creature, which is to 'gather what is scattered'. That is to say, by means of the spiritual way to leave multiplicity in order to re-enter Unity; to quit manifestation in order to return to its Principle; to

14. Simplicius, *Comment. on the Enchir.*, 7.

15. On the Odyssey: Lanoë-Villenne, *Le Livre des Symboles*, t. vi–2; G. Germain, *Genèse de l'Odyssee*; F. Buffière, *Les mythes d'Homère et la pensée grecque*. On the Argonauts, see Dante, *Paradiso* 33, 96; 2, 1–18); Apollonius of Rhodes, *Argonautica*. On the symbolism of the voyage in general, see R. Guénon, *Spiritual Authority and Temporal Power*, pp74–76.

abandon Time for Eternity. This is well expressed in the idea of 'peace' attached to both the sheepfold and the port; in the sheepfold, the sheep no longer run, just as in port the ship ceases to advance, and 'the soul that has God for shepherd possesses the One and Oneness, upon which the universe depends and, naturally, has no need of anything else.'[16]

The same meaning is conveyed by the geometric symbolism of center and circumference. The circumference designates the 'world', that is to say the 'dispersion' of the being in everything contingent, in action, and temporal life, whereas the immobile center signifies the return to the Principle, to God, contemplation, life eternal. The sheepfold and the port, which *gather*, are other images of the Center, contrasted to the voyage and grazing, which are images of the circumference that scatters. In this regard, it will be interesting to remember that at the end of the Flood, the Ark came to rest at the summit of Mount Ararat. This mountain is in fact one of the forms of the Cosmic Mountain, the mountain the flood never covers. In all traditions it rightly symbolizes the center of the world, the *Axis Mundi*, the point where man enters into communion with God, and where, escaping from the agitations of time, he is finally able to find rest, *requies aeterna*.[17]

16. Philo, op. cit. 54. In comparison, a Hindu teaching: 'It is you who, re-ascending the stream of ignorance with the raft of knowledge, has brought us across the current of *avidya*, whose sharks are birth, old age, sickness, and other evils, right to the other shore of this vast ocean, onto the firm ground of Deliverance, where one escapes from all return to the world of transmigration' (Commentary by Shankaracharya on the *Prashna Upanishad* 6, 4. tr. R. Allar, in ET 371 (1962), p140).

17. On the cosmic mountain: P. Gordon, *L'Image du monde dans l'antiquité*, pp14–42, and R. Guénon, *The King of the World*, pp46–57. On the Center: M. Eliade, *Patterns in Comparative Religion*, pp367 ff., *Images and Symbols*, pp27–56; R. Guénon, *Symbols of Sacred Science*, pp57–112, and our book on the Christian temple, *passim*.

9

God
the Fisherman
and God
the Hunter

ALONGSIDE the combination of shepherd and pilot is another symbolic scriptural pair, God the Fisherman and God the Hunter.

The first of this pair is clearly related to the nautical symbolism studied in the last chapter, and occupies as important a place in the New Testament as the image of the Good Shepherd. The account of the calling of the Apostles, of whom four of the twelve were fishermen, opens with a fishing scene: 'And Jesus said unto them, Come ye after me, and I will make you to become fishers of men' (Mark 1:17). To this should be added the account of the two miraculous catches (Luke 5; John 21), and, to a certain extent, the multiplication of the seven loaves and two fishes (Matt. 15:32–39). Thus it is not only the disciples who were fishers of men, but Christ Himself; He is, in a way, the 'prince of fishermen' as 'He is the prince of shepherds' (St Peter). The decorative art of the first centuries contains abundant examples of Him in this role. For example, at the mausoleum of the Julii, near the site of the Vatican's Constantinian basilica, we find a Christ seated at the edge of the water, pulling in his line with a fish attached to it.[1] Not only frescoes and reliefs, but also

---

1. Together in the same fresco are found a Christ-Sun, a Jonas, and a Good Shepherd (J. Carcopino, *Études d'hist. chrét.*, 1953, pp 151–152).

gems and engraved glasses, show Jesus both angling and fishing with a net, and himself carrying the catch.[2]

The religious literature echoes the figurative monuments. Clement of Alexandria introduces the theme in his Hymn to Christ:

> O Fisher of men whom you come to save, above the sea of vice you snatch pure fish; out of the hostile wave, you lead them to blessed life.[3]

It is taken up again in a different form in a hymn of the Syrian Nasrai: 'He (Jesus) has cast the net of His doctrine into the human sea, and in it has caught all the nations with their potentates.'[4] Among certain authors, like St Damasius, Christ is even compared to the net itself.[5] Nasrai's text seems to be inspired by a passage from the Old Testament, which he adapts to a new situation. In the Old Testament, the Lord is compared to a fisherman (and hunter), but is depicted here in the exercise of his vengeance against an unfaithful people.

> Behold, I shall send for many fishers, saith the Lord, and they shall fish them [the Children of Israel]; and after will I send for many hunters, and they shall hunt them from every mountain . . . and out of the holes of the rocks' (Jer. 16:16; cf. Amos 4:2).

There is also a passage from Habakkuk, of which Nasrai could well have been thinking, although he changes the spirit of the text, for Habakkuk's vengeful fishing of the Eternal becomes, with the Syrian, the merciful victory of the Son of Man. The Eternal, says the prophet,

> will make men as the fishes of the sea. . . . He lifted up all of them with his hook, he drew them in his seine, and gathered them into his net: for this he will be glad and rejoice. Therefore will he offer

---

2. See Charbonneau-Lassay, *Le Bestiare du Christ* (1940, reprint 1974), pp742 ff.

3. Clement of Alexandria, *Instructor, in fine*, v. 23–29.

4. *Homily on the Martyrs*, in OS 3–3 (1958), p304.

5. St Damasius, *Carm.*, vi. Cf. Ennodius, *Carm.*, i, 9; Orientus, according to Dom Martene-Durand, *Thesaurus anecdot.*, 5, 40.

victims to his seine, and he will sacrifice to his net (Hab. 1:14–16).

The avenging character, however, also appeared in another aspect of Christ the Fisherman, although somewhat different from what we have just seen, and not directly based on the New Testament. Here we have in mind Christ capturing the monster Leviathan, which, on the cosmological and theological planes respectively, simultaneously symbolizes chaos and Satan. St Cyril of Jerusalem tells us that at the time of His baptism in the Jordan, Christ

> of His own accord descended to the place where the invisible whale of death is, so that death vomited up those it had swallowed, in conformity with Scripture: 'Thou brakest the heads of the dragons in the waters. Thou brakest the head of leviathan in pieces' (Psalm 73).[6]

Likewise in St Catherine of Siena, God, alluding to the Incarnation, says: 'It is with the bait of your humanity and the hook of My divinity that I have caught the Demon.'[7] This image of God the Fisherman is the exact analogue of that of God transfixing Rahab, the former on the plane of aquatic and halieutic symbolism, and the latter on that of warrior symbolism.[8]

This theme inspired Christian iconography: the image of Christ capturing Leviathan can be seen in a Roman catacomb[9] and in a mural in a church in Aquileia.[10] In one of the vignettes of the famous *Hortus deliciarum* of the Abbess Herrad of Landsberg, Leviathan, the dragon of the sea, can be seen with its mouth caught on a hook that forms the lower end of the Cross; the latter is attached to a line fixed to a fishing rod held by Christ, who is standing above the monster.[11]

6. St Cyril of Jerusalem, *Mystagogical Catechesis*, xiv, 17.
7. This is to say that in the Word, humanity was the bait and the divinity the hook (St Cath. of Sienna, *Dialog.*, chap. 135).
8. See above, chap. 3.
9. DAC 64, 2034.
10. Reproduced in L. Charbonneau-Lassay, *Le Bestiare du Christ*, p747.
11. Reproduced in M.M. Davy, *La Symbolique romane*, 1955, p174.

The fisherman's net is closely related to that of the hunter. The latter instrument of capture, together with the lasso which binds and chokes the prey, is a fairly frequent image in the Bible. Furthermore, they are both ambivalent images, expressing not only God's action, but also that of sickness, death and the devil: 'The sorrows of hell compassed me about; the snares of death prevented me' (2 Sam. 22:6). 'The sorrows of death compassed me, and the pains of hell got hold upon me: I found trouble and sorrow. Then called I upon the name of the Lord; O Lord, I beseech thee deliver my soul' (Psalm 116; cf. Psalm 18).

Death is thus considered a power of the devil, and the same applies to sickness. In the New Testament, in particular, a sick person is considered to be 'bound' by the devil. Such was the case with the woman who had been sick for eighteen years, whom Jesus healed on the Sabbath. To the reproaches of the Jews that He did not respect the Lord's Day, Jesus answered: 'And ought not this woman, being a daughter of Abraham, whom *Satan hath bound*, lo, these eighteen years, be loosed from this bond on the Sabbath day?' (Luke 13:16). Like physical sickness, sickness of the soul—sin—is a fall into the nets of Satan: 'Those who would be rich, fall into temptation and the toils of the Devil....' (1 Tim. 3:7). Sinners should 'wake up, that they may recover themselves out of the snare of the devil, who are taken captive by him at his will' (2 Tim. 2:26).

But the Devil, after all, only acts with God's permission, and we should not be surprised to see the very symbols of the chase and the capture serving to translate an aspect of divine activity. If the tender images of the Good Shepherd, and sometimes even the images of the Fisherman, express the working of His clemency and mercy, those of the Hunter tell of the working of His justice and rigor. In short, we are brought very close to a divine aspect studied at the beginning of this book: God the Hunter very much resembles God the Warrior.

The Lord is the master of the bonds of death. The prophets show Him, net in hand, pursuing the guilty: 'My net also will I spread upon him ... and I will bring him to Babylon' (Ezek. 12:13 and 17:20). 'I will therefore spread out my net over thee....' (ibid., 32:3). With Job, the hunter's nets symbolize omnipotence: 'Know now that

God hath overthrown me, and hath compassed me with his net' (Job 19:6). If the wicked also spread nets, God uses them to capture the guilty themselves: 'The heathen are sunk down in the pit that they made: in the net, which they hid, is their own foot taken. The Lord is known by the judgment which he executeth: the wicked is snared in the work of his own hands' (Psalm 9).

It seems that here we may well be faced with a typically Semitic symbolism. If, in fact, God has been seen nearly everywhere as having the traits of a hunter,[12] for example in India, where Varuna is a 'master of the bonds', who 'imprisons the wicked in his snares', and 'binds' and 'unbinds' men at a distance,[13] it nevertheless remains true that God the hunter occupies a privileged place in the myths of Mesopotamia and Syria, the influence of which on the form of certain books of the Bible we are well aware. Thus, the gods Enzil (and Ninlil), and Enzu capture perjurers in their nets;[14] Shamash, the Sun, has snares and ropes: prayers are addressed to him for the freeing of captives. The goddess Nisaba, for her part, binds the demons of sickness. Another god, Marduk, is also a master 'binder'; he fights the monster Tiamat, that is to say Chaos, binds and chains it, and tears out its life. Then he chains the gods and demons that helped Tiamat and casts them into the nets and fish-traps. Likewise, the god Tammuz (Adonis) is called 'Lord of the nets'.[15]

What we have here are obviously cosmogonic myths, analogous to those of the destruction of Rahab and Leviathan in the Bible, and of Python by the solar Apollo of Delphi. These myths can also be given a moral interpretation, the chaos represented by the monsters in question designating disorder on every level.

As the emblem of Omnipotence, the image of the net can assume an imposing appearance and an unsuspected importance, as for example in these texts of Rabbi Akibah: 'A net is spread over all living creatures,' and Meister Eckhart: 'God has cast His net and lasso

---

12. M. Eliade, 'The "God who Binds"' in *Images and Symbols*, pp92–124.

13. Ibid., p96. Athena, too, caused Ajax, whom she wished to punish for his pride, to fall into 'her mortal toils' (Sophocles, *Ajax*, 59–60).

14. Ibid., p142.

15. Ibid., p143. — He is also called 'good shepherd' (Ch. Autran, *Préhistoire du christianisme*, I, p171).

over all creatures, in such a way that it can be discovered and recognized in each of them.'[16] In striking fashion, the symbol here expresses the very condition of man and of every creature in the world, a condition in which it is impossible for them in any way to escape God.

To become aware of this situation and perhaps to accept it can be, moreover, the starting point of the spiritual path, which explains how such a path may sometimes be compared to a hunt in which the soul is, as it were, 'being tracked' by God,[17] or, inversely, is 'ardently hunting its prey, Christ' (Eckhart). We ought to pursue the development of this final metaphor in the writings of spiritual authors, but this would exceed the limits of the present study.

---

16. *Pirke Aboth*, 3, 20: Eckhart, *Sermons*, no. 69.

17. This is the subject of the poem by Francis Thompson, *The Hound of Heaven*, in which the heavenly Hound is seen in tireless pursuit of man.

10

The
Celestial
Gardener

BEFORE BECOMING, like many other things in the modern world, a simple utility, a 'green space', or purely an amusement, the garden, along with the house and the temple, was always considered by civilized peoples to be an image of the world.

Such was the case with the Persian garden, so famous throughout the ancient world. At the time of the Sassanids, when it reached its full development, it was rectangular in shape and divided into four parts by two main axes in the form of a cross that emphasized a path or a watercourse. At its center, where the two axes crossed, was the prince's palace, a pavilion, or fountain. This layout corresponded to the scheme of the universe divided into four zones by four great rivers. The famous 'paradise' of Cyrus at Sardis, described by Xenophon,[1] expressed this idea of a universe with the King's (magus') palace at its center representing the fecund and creative power of nature. The Persian garden was a microcosm surrounding a princely residence; it was like a sacred wood where the fundamental elements of the universe converged.[2] This cosmic scheme was

---

1. Xenophon, *Econom.* 4, 21. — It is known that the word 'paradise' is Persian, coming, via the Greek *paradison*, from the Persian *paradesha*.
2. P. Grimal, *L'Art des jardins* (1954), pp 20–21, 39, 41, 43. — The layout of the Persian garden, with its four axes and the royal palace at the center, obviously derives from a conception parallel to that of the Chinese *Ming Tang*, where the King-Pontiff regenerated his empire through the stations at the cardinal points in

perpetuated in Europe, with variations, until the classical epoch. It is what still gives Versailles its incomparable meaning.[3]

But if the garden is an image of the world, the world in its turn can be seen as a garden, with God the Creator as the Gardener who conceived, designed, realized, and planted it at the beginning, and whose Providence continues to care for it throughout the course of time: 'I have come to the world,' says the Gardener, 'to plant the plantation of life.'[4]

The original world was the Garden of Eden, the earthly paradise:

And the Lord planted a garden eastward in Eden, and there he put the man whom he had formed. And out of the ground made the Lord God to grow every tree that is pleasant to the sight and good for food; the tree of life also in the midst of the garden, and the tree of knowledge of good and evil. And a river went out of Eden to water the garden, and from thence it was parted, and became into four heads. The name of the first is Pison: that is it which compasseth the whole land of Havilah, where there is gold, and the gold of that land is good. There is bdellium and the onyx stone. And the name of the second river is Gihon: the same is it that compasseth the whole land of Ethiopia. And the name of the third river is Hiddekel: that is it which goeth toward the east of Assyria. And the fourth river is Euphrates. And the Lord God took the man, and put him into the garden of Eden to dress it and to keep it (Gen. 2:8–15).

And God, like a master craftsman happy with his creation, 'walked in the garden in the cool of the day' (Gen. 3:8).

It will have been noted that the shape of paradise corresponds to that of the Persian garden with its four cardinal axes embodied in the watercourses.

---

order to 'inaugurate the seasons', and then at the center of the palace in order, as the Mover of the Year, to authoritatively animate Space and Time (M. Granet, *La Pensée chinoise*, 1950), pp 102–3.

3. On the symbolism of the park at Versailles: Ed. Guillou, *Versailles palais du soleil* (1963).

4. *Book of John* (Lidbarsky, p 219). This is one of the Mandaean books.

The future paradise, the world Beyond, appeared with the same traits among both the Greeks and Egyptians, to confine ourselves to these two examples. For Homer, *Elysium* is a plain without winter, where fresh breezes always blow; likewise, the *Isle of the Blessed* evoked by Pindar, in a veritable mystical frenzy, is the land 'refreshed by sea breezes, where flowers of gold shine, some on land, on the boughs of magnificent trees, others floating on the waters.'[5] In Egypt, the *Field of Iaru* is a garden overflowing with greenery and water where the blessed feed on the fruit of the tree of life;[6] which is a conception curiously close to that of Aphraates the Syrian, who describes the dwelling place of Christian souls as follows:

> The air is pleasant and serene, a brilliant light shines, trees grow whose fruit ripens perpetually, of which the leaves never fall, and beneath these shades ... the souls eat this fruit.[7]

But paradise is already virtually realized by the Redemption of Christ, who has renewed and restored the world. Clement of Alexandria magnificently explicates the text from Genesis in this way:

> Now Moses, describing allegorically the divine prudence, called it the tree of life planted in Paradise; which Paradise may be the world in which all things proceeding from creation grow. In it also the Word blossomed and bore fruit, being 'made flesh', and gave life to those 'who had tasted of His graciousness.'[8]

The Christian and Paschal mystery is that of the return of humanity to Paradise from which it had been banished.[9] Thus we see the Fathers emphasizing the striking parallel that exists between the Garden of Eden and the gardens that were the theater of the Redemption: the Garden of Gethsemane and the garden of Joseph

---

5. *Odyssey*, IV, 563–9; Pindar, *Olymp.*, II, 77 ff.

6. Erman, *Religion des Egyptiens* (Fr. transl. pp 251–2). Cf. *Livre des Morts* (Naville, 59, 63).

7. Cited in F. Cumont, *After Life in Roman Paganism* (reprinted, Kessinger Publishing, 2003), p 206.

8. Clement of Alexandria, *Stromata* V, 11.

9. See J. Daniélou, *Catéchèse pascale et retour au paradis*, in MD 45 (1956), pp 99–119.

of Arimathea. 'In Paradise,' says St Cyril of Jerusalem, 'was the fall, and in a garden our salvation. From the tree came sin, and until the Tree sin lasted.'[10] The same idea is found many centuries later in St Catherine of Siena:

> I created the rational creatures in my own image and likeness, and I put them in this garden. But because of Adam's sin the garden where first there were fragrant flowers, innocently pure and so very sweet, brought forth thorns. . . . [But Christ came and] I made the earth a garden watered by the blood of Christ crucified, and planted there the seven gifts of the Holy Spirit. . . .[11]

The hill of Golgotha, where the Tree of the Cross, the new Tree of Life, was planted, has been assimilated to Paradise regained. Moreover, in iconography as in Christian literature, the blood of the Crucified One, the fountain of life, has been represented as flowing in the four directions of space, like the rivers of Eden.[12]

Less attention is given to the garden adjoining Golgotha, where Joseph of Arimathea hollowed out of rock the sepulcher used for the Lord (John 19:41). Nothing is without importance in Holy Scripture, however; as we have already had occasion to observe, the least detail is full of meaning.[13] Such is the case here. The appearance of the risen Christ to Mary Magdalen in this garden replicates the scene of Eve's temptation in the original garden, as St Hippolytus of Rome saw clearly: 'Eve in the garden of temptation heralds Magdalen in the garden of the resurrection.'[14] The wealth of meaning revealed by this exegesis invites us to stretch the parallel: this garden symbolizes the world regenerated by the victory of Christ over death, paradise regained. And as if that were not sufficient for our understanding, the inspired author takes care to tell us that

---

10. *Mystagogical Catechesis*, 13, 19.

11. *The Dialogue*, chap. 140; tr. S. Noffke (NY: Paulist Press, 1980), p288.

12. We have dealt with the cruci-circular pattern forming the basis of these representations in our book *The Symbolism of the Christian Temple*, in particular, pp14–21, 81, 157 ff.

13. See above pp 12–13.

14. *Cant. d. cant.* (Boutwetsch, p352).

Magdalen at first took Jesus for 'the gardener' (John 20:15). This little touch, which could pass as a simple realistic detail at the hand of the sacred historian, assumes a completely different meaning the moment it is placed in the symbolic context under analysis. Here, Christ reveals Himself to Magdalen and to us in his function as Divine Gardener, as the One who has come to restore the Garden of the World.

This parallel between the Gardens of Eden and the Redemption is subject to an extension in the historical order. It is found in St Bernard, who compares the spiritual history of the world with the life of a garden that unfolds in three phases: creation, reconciliation, and reparation. The first period is like the sowing and planting of the garden. The second is like the germination of the seeded and planted soil: 'For in due course, while the heavens showered from above and the skies rained down the Just one, the earth opened for a Savior to spring up' (Isaiah 45:8). The third, finally, will come at the end of time, when 'the good will be gathered from the midst of the wicked, like fruit from a garden, to be set at rest in the storehouse of God.' 'In that day,' says Isaiah (4:2), 'the branch of the Lord shall be beautiful and glorious, and the fruit of the land raised on high.'[15]

Let us note in passing that in its eschatological perspective, this symbol is not ignored by Muslim mystics, who say that at the end of the world, 'the garden will return to the Gardener,' that is to say, the created to the Creator.[16]

But, concretely, the spiritual history of the world is the history of the Church of Christ. The Church also is compared to a garden and the faithful to the verdant trees growing there.

The fundamental elements of this theme are fully expounded by St Ephrem:

God planted the fair garden, He built the pure Church. . . . In the Church He planted the Word. . . . The assembly of saints bears

---

15. Sermon 23 in *On the Song of Songs II*, tr. K. Walsh (Kalamazoo, MI: Cistercian Publications, 1976), p29; PL 183, 884–894.

16. F. Schuon, 'Comments on an Eschatological Problem', in *Form and Substance in the Religions* (Bloomington, Indiana: World Wisdom, 2002), p238.

resemblance to Paradise: in it each day is plucked the fruit of Him who gives life to all. . . .[17]

With Sts Cyprian and Hippolytus the symbol is enriched with an allusion to the river of life divided into four branches:

> The Church, like Paradise, includes fruit-bearing trees within her walls. . . . She waters the trees from four rivers, which are the four gospels, by which she dispenses the grace of baptism by means of a celestial and salutary outpouring.[18]

> The Church, God's spiritual garden, planted in Christ as in the East: here may be seen every sort of tree [patriarchs, prophets, etc.]. An inexhaustible river flows through this garden, and from it four streams water the whole earth. So it is with the Church. Christ is the river, and he is proclaimed in the world by the four gospels. . . .[19]

In the last passage, we see taking shape the motif of the righteous as verdant trees, a motif that has great scope, being inspired by the Psalms. Thus, in his *Nocturne,* Isaac of Antioch paraphrases Psalm 92:

> The righteous man will flourish like the palm, and grow like the cedar of Lebanon, whose leaves never fall, whose splendor never fades. He is planted in the House of the Lord and the courts of our God, where the Spirit blows and intoxicates him with its breath. Through the action of the Holy Spirit he thrives and grows tall like the cedar of Lebanon. Even in old age he bears fruit, for the sacred chants give him youth; he is full of vigor and grace, because he has understood the mysteries of the Spirit.[20]

---

17. St Ephrem the Syrian, *Hymns on Paradise,* 6, 7–9, tr. S. Beck (Crestwood, NY: St Vladimir's Seminary Press, 1990), p111.

18. St Cyprian, *Letters.,* 73, 10.

19. St Hippolytus, *Commentary on Daniel,* 1, 17; cited in J. Daniélou, *Primitive Christian Symbols,* p30.

20. G. Bickell, *Ausg. Gedichte der Syr. Kirchenvater,* pp164–170. The title of John Moschos' work, *The Spiritual Meadow,* is explained along the same lines; see his preface (tr. J. Wortley [Kalamazoo, MI: Cistercian Publications, 1992], p3).

St Bernard, at the other end of Christianity, expresses himself no differently: 'We find men of many virtues, like fruitful trees in the garden of the Bridegroom, in the Paradise of God.' The good man is a plant of God: 'And he shall be like a tree planted by the rivers of water, that bringeth forth his fruit in his season; his leaf also shall not wither' (Psalm 1:3). And Jeremiah: 'For he shall be as a tree planted by the waters, that spreadeth out her roots by the river, and shall not notice when heat cometh'(17:8). 'The righteous shall flourish like the palm tree; he shall grow like a cedar in Lebanon' (Psalm 91). 'But I am like a green olive in the house of God' (Psalm 50).[21]

This theme is very ancient. From the early years of Christianity, the Church was called 'the plantation (*phytia*) of God'; the faithful are the trees that the Heavenly Gardener has planted there. In the *Teaching of the Apostles* we read, 'The catholic Church is God's plantation.'[22] St Paul had already compared baptism to a plantation, since he called the newly initiated, *neophyte*, which means 'new plant' (1 Tim. 3:6). Clement of Alexandria explains it thus:

Our gnosis and our spiritual paradise itself are the Savior, in whom we are planted, being transferred and transplanted from the old life to the good earth. And the change of plantation is accompanied by the production of much fruit.[23]

The image lived on into the Middle Ages. Thus St Catherine of Siena wrote to Pope Urban VI: 'The Eternal Truth desires that in your Garden, you make a garden of God's servants. . . .'; and again: 'It is necessary . . . to renew the Garden of Holy Church.'[24] It even inspires a work like the *Romance of the Rose*, which is not religious, at least directly. This book presents us with two contrasted gardens, that of carnal pleasures and that of Beatitude, the only true garden of delights, wherein the Lamb of God leads the sheep in meadows of

21. St Bernard, op. cit., p 28.

22. *Teaching of the Apostles* cited in J. Daniélou, *Primitive Christian Symbols*, p 27. The image is particularly developed in the text of Qumran, ibid., and G. Bernini, *Il Giardiniere della piantgione eternal* in *Sacra Pagina* II (Louvain, 1959), pp 47–49.

23. Clement of Alexandria, *Stromata* IV, 1, 4.

24. J. Leclerq, *Ste Catherine de Sienne*, pp 105, 100, 116.

eternal flowers. There they find the Fountain of Life in which an olive tree, symbolizing Grace, bathes its roots, and in which shines the sparkling carbuncle of the Beatific Vision.[25] This image is not unrelated to that of Dante, who describes the world of the Blessed as forming an immense Rose in the garden of the Eternal Fountain.[26]

The scriptural comparison of man to a tree planted in the Garden of God, starting with the Man-God assimilated to the Tree of Life, finds an echo in the work of Plato. According to him,

> We are a plant not of an earthly but of a heavenly growth (*phyton ouranion*) . . . for the divine power suspends the head and root of us from that place where the generation of the soul first began, and thus makes the entire body upright.[27]

A different, and in a way inverse, form of this symbol was destined to enjoy considerable success: we have in mind the mandrake. This magic plant, which had a root but no head, did not symbolize the descent of man from heaven to earth, as did the Platonic plant, of which the root was a head, but rather his re-ascension to heaven. Just as the dark root, subject to Hecate but collected by the wise botanist, becomes a saving remedy, so the dark root of human nature, subjected to demons, becomes salutary, because the eternal Herbalist knows how to transform it by freeing it from the bonds of Satan. The poisoned root, similar to a man without a head, is crowned with eternal rest in Christ, who is the head of all.[28]

Botanical speculations of this sort, together with those centered on the Greek pharmacopoeia, are based on a passage from the Song

---

25. *The Romance of the Rose*, tr. C. Dahlberg (Princeton, NJ: Princeton University Press, 1983), v. 19, 932–20, 655, pp 328–337.

26. *Paradiso*, 31. — The poet Sedulius had already placed the rose in the earthly Paradise, and Prudence and St Peter Damian in the Paradise to come. Cf. Ch. Joret, *La rose dans l'Antiquité et au Moyen Age*, pp 229–237.

27. Plato, *Timaeus* 90A–B. The expression was adopted by Plutarch, *De Pythiae oraculis*, 12 and *Anthology*, 10, 45.

28. See H. Rahner, *The Mandrake…* in *Greek Myths and Christian Mysteries*, pp 223–277.

of Solomon, which is closely related to the symbolism of the garden, as shall be immediately evident. St Gregory the Great writes:

The mandrakes spread their perfume (7:14). By the root of the mandrake we may understand the nature of man. . . . Even as a root ages in the ground and gradually begins to die, so it is with man, who, according to the nature of his flesh, resolves himself at last into ashes. The root becomes dust, and the beauty of the man's body suffers corruption. But the fragrance of the living water causes the root to revive, and similarly the human body is recreated when the Holy Spirit descends.[29]

The dark root is nostalgic for the light, and from a headless root the fragrant efflorescence of Eternity unfolds.[30]

These reflections on the human plant and the mandrake have already taken us from the domain of the cosmic and ecclesiastic symbolism of gardens into its microcosmic symbolism, and here we shall pause by way of ending. After the gardens of the world and the Church, we shall consider the garden of the soul.

'The human soul has become a garden full of sweet and exquisite fruits,' says St Catherine of Siena,[31] echoing the *Letter to Diognetus*:

Those who truly love God become a paradise of delights; a fruit-bearing tree of vigorous sap springs up in them, and they are adorned with the richest fruits.'[32]

---

29. St Gregory the Great, *Moralia in Job*, 12, 5, 7; cited in Rahner, ibid., p 248. One also finds the mandrake in *Genesis*, 30:14; and the *Song of Solomon*, 7:13. According to Richard of St Victor, it denotes good repute, renown.

30. In Rahner's excellent study are found all the variations on the theme with citations of texts (Origen, Philo of Karpasia, Nilus of Ancyra, etc...), as well as a rich bibliography on the question. These texts can be compared to the following passage from the Quran (50, 9–11): 'We have caused the blessed water to descend from heaven and through it have caused gardens and the grain of the harvest to grow. . . . And through it we have revived a dead land. Such is the Resurrection.' Likewise, in the Jewish tradition, it is said that a dew will come forth from the head of the Ancient of Days to revive the dead in the ages to come. (H. Serouya, *La Kabbale*, p 287). Cf. St Paul, 1 Cor. 15:36–38 and 42–44, and below, chap. 11.

31. St Catherine of Siena, *Dialogues*, chap. 140.

32. *Letter to Diognetus*, 12, 1–3.

The idea of a garden of the soul arises naturally from Scripture. Jeremiah, recalling the restoration of the earthly Paradise on the Mount Sion of the Apocalypses, notes its prolongations in the human soul, which will then reflect the peace and joy of Eden.

> The Lord hath redeemed Jacob, and ransomed him from the hand of him that was stronger than he. Therefore they shall come and sing in the height of Zion, and shall flow together to the goodness of the Lord, for wheat, and for wine, and for oil, and for the young of the flock and of the herd: and their soul shall be as a watered garden; and they shall not sorrow any more at all (Jer. 31:11–12; see also Isaiah 58:9).

Philo interprets the verse: 'And Noah began to be a husbandman. . . .' (Gen. 9:20), allegorically in the same sense. By this, he says, we are to understand the cultivation of the soul (*georgiki psychis*), which consists in pulling out the trees of folly and the passions, and planting the good trees of the virtues.[33]

But it is above all the garden of the *Song of Solomon* that is considered to be the symbol of the soul. At times this garden is the place of the mystical marriage of the Word and the soul, represented by the Beloved and the Spouse, and at others, the Soul itself.[34] There we find the splendid evocation of the sealed garden, the image of the pure soul filled with the perfume of all the virtues; without a doubt, poetry has never attained such grace and charm. 'A garden inclosed is my sister, my spouse; a spring shut up, a fountain sealed. Thy plants are an orchard of pomegranates, with pleasant fruits; camphire, with spikenard, spikenard and saffron; calamus and cinnamon, with all trees of frankincense; myrrh and aloes, with all the chief spices: a fountain of gardens, a well of living water, and streams from Lebanon' (Song of Sol. 4:12–15).[35] The Beloved enters

---

33. Philo, *De agricul.*, 7, 25.

34. On the development of this theme in patristic literature, especially in St Cyril of Jerusalem and St Ambrose, see J. Daniélou, *The Bible and the Liturgy*, pp191–207.

35. According to traditional exegesis, fruit trees symbolized charity, scented trees the virtue of religion, and resinous trees renunciation (Abbé Geslin, *Le Cantique des cantiques*, pp91–92).

his garden; and so the dialogue is established between him and the soul-spouse, in which the praise of the delights of this garden unfolds in endless arabesques.

Let my beloved come into his garden and eat his pleasant fruits. I am come into my garden, my sister, my spouse; I have gathered my myrrh with my spice; I have eaten my honeycomb with my honey; I have drunk my wine with my milk.... My beloved is gone down into his garden, to the beds of spices, to feed in the gardens, and to gather lilies (5:1; 6:2).

In the autobiography of St Teresa of Avila, the theme of Solomon's garden served as the framework for a whole mystical treatise on the states of prayer.[36] There we read that the mystical soul is comparable to a garden. A beginner in the spiritual life 'must look upon himself as making a garden, wherein our Lord may take His delight.' (We recognize the plot of the *Song of Solomon*.)

His Majesty roots up the weeds, and has to plant good herbs ... as good gardeners, by the help of God, to see that the plants grow, to water them carefully, that they may not die, but produce blossoms, which shall send forth much fragrance, refreshing to our Lord, so that He may come often for His pleasure into this garden, and delight Himself in the midst of these virtues.

How is the garden to be watered? In four ways: first, with water drawn from wells by the strength of one's arms; secondly, with the help of the Persian wheel; thirdly, by irrigation; and, finally, by leaving it to the rain, when it is then the Lord Himself who waters. These four ways of watering correspond to the four types of prayer. Our Lord is the 'master of the garden', while the beginner is a gardener, and the four ways of watering are prescribed by the master of the garden. The flowers grow; God gives them a lovely scent; He cuts them, He hoes and removes the weeds. In the third way of watering, the prayer of quietude, God takes the place of the gardener and He Himself, the Heavenly Gardener, does the watering (chaps. 16 and 17): in an instant, through the water of Grace, He is

---

36. *Life, Written by Herself,* chaps. 11–20.

able to make the fruit grow and ripen. Finally, in the fourth way, the prayer of union, it is the heavenly rain that falls and soaks the garden. The water that falls is the grace of union (chap. 18), which falls from 'the Cloud of the Divine Majesty itself' (chap. 20).

At the end of the treatise, we see how the great mystic, in celebrating the marriage of the Soul and the Word, quite naturally rejoins the tremendous vision of the Incarnation in Isaiah: 'Drop down dew, ye heavens, from above, and let the clouds rain the just: let the earth be opened, and bud forth a savior' (45:8).

Garden of the world, garden of the Church, garden of the soul: works of the same and unique 'Principle of every sowing', of the one and only 'Gardener of all spiritual growth'.[37]

---

37. Ancient liturgical prayer: *Berlin Papyrus* (Egypt second cent.), PO 18, 430.

11

The Master
of the Harvest

'WORKS AND DAYS...' More than any other, this expression of the
aged peasant poet Hesiod recalls the very web of our life. Agricultural work, noble because in accord with natural laws and rhythms,
is admirably suited to helping us discern the divine activity in the
world. The cultivation of wheat and vine, bread and wine, are pow-
erful symbols that God invites us to venerate and ponder, seeing
that He made them supports of His mysterious presence among us.

If the world is a garden in which God lets beings bloom, it is also
a field in which He sows them, and a vineyard in which he plants
them.

Scripture teaches us that God is a *farmer*, 'Pater meus est agri-
cola,' says Jesus (John 15:1). 'Every plant, which my heavenly Father
hath not planted, shall be rooted up' (Matt. 15:13). Elsewhere, He
calls His Father the 'Lord of the Harvest' (Luke 10:2).

These assertions should be understood initially in a literal sense.
It is obvious to every normal person that the riches of the earth, like
the art of cultivation, are gifts of God; man would know nothing
about agriculture if God had not taught him. 'It is God who teaches
the husbandman his skills' (Isaiah 28:24–29). We have explained
above, regarding architecture, how this type of expression should be
understood.

Better still: the peasant is only an instrument in the hand of God;
the movements of a man at work are only the external manifestation of work carried on by God. It is God who brings forth the pastures and causes the fields of wheat to grow:

Thou hast visited the earth, and hast plentifully watered it; thou hast many ways enriched it. The river of God is filled with water, thou hast prepared their food: for so is its preparation. Fill up plentifully the streams thereof, multiply its fruits; it shall spring up and rejoice in its showers. Thou shalt bless the crown of the year of thy goodness: and thy fields shall be filled with plenty. The beautiful places of the wilderness shall grow fat: and the hills shall be girded about with joy (Psalm 64:10–13).

According to the prophet, the Lord 'shall come unto us as the rain, as the latter and the former rain unto the earth,' and His 'goodness is as a morning cloud, and as the early dew it goeth away' (Hos. 6:3–4).

After the harvest, in the month of *tisri* (September), the Hebrews celebrated the Feast of Tabernacles to give thanks to God for His blessings. 'Seven days shalt thou keep a solemn feast unto the Lord thy God in the place which the Lord shall choose: because the Lord thy God shall bless thee in all thine increase' (Deut. 16:15).

Comparable feasts and rites have existed amongst all peoples, moreover. The Greeks had the Thalysia and the Thesmophoria, and the Romans the *messium feriae*. In Christian lands, while faith was still alive, people thought and acted in the same way. The Feast of the Rogations, was scrupulously celebrated, while all sorts of para-liturgical rites surrounding the last sheaf expressed the peasants' faith in and acknowledgment of God. In Berry and Perigord, when the harvest was finished, a pole was erected supporting a cross made from ears of corn, around which people sang and danced; at many places, the first-fruits of the wheat were presented to the Virgin.[1] All

---

1. On the Jewish feasts, see for example K. Hruby, *Shavuôt ou la Pentecôte*, which assembles the scriptural texts, in OS 8–3 and 4 (1963), pp395–412. On the popular traditions of France, M. Vloberg, *Fêtes de France, passim*. On the sacredness of agricultural work, M. Eliade, *Patterns of Comparative Religion*, pp331–349. The old belief that it is principally the divinity who is at work in agriculture is well-attested, for example, among the Greeks. There, Zeus is called *ombrios*, 'he who gives the rain', Poseidon, *phytalmion*, 'he who causes growth', Demeter, *proerosia*, 'she whom one evokes before ploughing' (Plutarch, *Banquet of the Seven Wise Men*, 15). This invocation of Demeter took place during a sacrifice accompanied with prayers, which inaugurated the ploughing, and even bore the name of *ta proerosia* (DAGR, s.v.).

these agrarian liturgies aimed at highlighting the sacredness of the work of the fields. There is, in fact, something sacred about vegetation, and man, by means of agricultural work, comes into contact with the mystery of life and its elaboration.

This presence of the divine in the life of earth and plant explains how the latter can be a preferred symbol of supernatural life, a symbol that Jesus often used in his preaching to enlighten His disciples on the nature of the Kingdom of God.

God is the Sower, and the seed He sows is His Word: 'Behold there went out a sower to sow....The sower soweth the word' (Mark 4:3–20). The Pseudo-Chrysostomus comments on this passage as follows: 'The Sower is Christ; the seed is the Divine Word; the field is humanity; the oxen, the apostles; the plough, the cross; the yoke, concord....'[2] Here we have the working out of a very diverse symbolism, certain elements of which we will find among other authors. St Ambrose called the Apostles the 'sowers of the faith', *satores fidei*.[3] Already St Paul had written to the Corinthians: 'I have planted, Apollos watered; but God gave the increase.... For we are laborers together with God: ye are God's husbandry, *Dei agricultura estis*' (1 Cor. 3:6–9). As to the plough, Christ evoked it in relation to the apostolic work: 'No man having put his hand to the plough, and looking back, is fit for the Kingdom of God' (Luke 9:62). Around the image of the plough, the Fathers developed that of Christ the ploughman. Thus Clement of Alexandria called Him *aroter*.[4] The point of departure is the messianic prophecy of Isaiah announcing that, at the reestablishment of the Kingdom, men 'shall beat their swords into ploughshares and their spears into pruning-hooks' (2:3–4). 'Our Lord Himself,' says St Irenaeus,

has made the plough and brought the pruning-hook: this designates the first sowing of man, which was his modeling on Adam, and the gathering of the harvest by the Word in the last times. . . .

2. PG 61, 773.
3. St Ambrose, V *in Lucam*, 44.
4. Clement of Alexandria, *Instructor, in fine: Hymn to Christ*, v. 19.

At the end, the Lord manifested the plough, wood joined to iron, and in this way weeded His soil. In fact, the sturdy Word, united with the flesh and fastened to it, has cleared the wasteland.[5]

St Ephrem expresses the same idea: 'The field of Christ is cultivated; no weeds can grow there; it is ploughed with the plough of the cross and its thorn-bushes are entirely rooted out.'[6]

The symbolism of God the ploughman and sower must have played a very important role in early catechesis, seeing that it is found in the famous magic square composed of the following text, arranged crosswise: *Sator arepo tenet opera rotas.*[7] J. Carcopino, who studied it following a great many others, proposes the following translation: 'The Sower, alert at his plough, carefully guides its wheels,' and shows that this enigmatic formula designates Christ. The word *sator* already served in classical Latin to translate the idea of the divinity as creator. It appears with the same meaning later on in Boethius.

O You, who govern the world through your eternal Reason, sower of lands and of heaven, who since the beginning of the ages have charge of the march of time and remain immovable in the midst of the movements You imprint upon the universe. . . .[8]

Much earlier, Plato showed God sowing the souls of the creatures in the earth.[9] In its most universal meaning, this symbol designates the Logos, the creator of all beings. 'God . . . sows the cosmic possi-

---

5. *Adv. haeres.*, 4, 34, 4.

6. St Ephrem, *On the Resurrection of Lazarus*, II (*Bibl. d. Kirchenvater*, 37, 176). — The assimilation of the cross to a plough is explained by the shape the latter had in Greek antiquity (see DAGR–1, 353).

7. J. Carcopino, *Etudes d'hist. chrét., Le Christianisme secrète du carré magique,* 1953, pp 11–91 and the reflections of G. Germain, *Contemplation et interpretation du Carré magique*, in *Bull. Assoc. G. Budé*, 1966–1.

8. Boethius, III, 9. Cf. Hymn of Lauds for the Feast of St Michael (29 Sept.): *Christe, gentis humanae sator.*

9. *Timaeus* 42D. The image enjoyed great success in Stoicism which spread the doctrine of the 'seminal ideas' (*logoi spermatikoi*) or generative ideas of things and beings. See Diogenes Laertius, 7, 448; Marcus Aurelius, 6, 24. Likewise, there is this beautiful formula in Cicero: 'The immortal gods have sown souls in the bodies of men' (*De senect.*, 21, 77).

bilities in *Materia prima*';[10] it is this latter ontological and cosmological reality that *terra mater* represents on the physical plane,
opening herself under the share of the plough to gather the seeds of
plants as well as the rain of heaven, another form of the Divine
Activity lauded by Isaiah in the magnificent text cited at the end of
the previous chapter.

In the Gospel parables, the phases in the life of the wheat and the
phases of agricultural work express the phases of the life of the
Kingdom and the stages of salvation.

> So is the kingdom of God, as if a man should cast seed into the
> ground . . . and the seed should spring and grow up. . . . For the
> earth bringeth forth fruit of herself; first the blade, then the ear,
> after that the full corn in the ear. But when the fruit is brought
> forth, immediately he putteth in the sickle, because the harvest is
> come (Mark 4:26–29).

The theme of the harvest assumes special importance, for it has
an eschatological meaning: in the history of salvation, the harvest is
the Judgment. Jesus tells us, moreover, that while the Sower (God)
slept, His Enemy (the devil) sowed tares that sprang up together
with the wheat. Both are left to grow until the harvest, when they
are separated, the good seed being brought in, and the tares burnt
(Matt. 13). The scene of God the Harvester is treated in magisterial
fashion in the Apocalypse (14:14ff.):

> And behold a white cloud, and upon the cloud one sat like unto
> the Son of man, having on his head a golden crown, and in his
> hand a sharp sickle. And another angel came out of the temple,
> crying with a loud voice to him that sat on the cloud, Thrust in
> thy sickle, and reap: for the time has come for thee to reap, for
> the harvest of the earth is ripe. And he that sat on the cloud
> thrust in his sickle on the earth; and the earth was reaped.

10. F. Schuon, *Stations of Wisdom*, (Bloomington, IN: World Wisdom Books,
1995), p129.

A parallel theme, related to the separation of the good and the wicked, is that of winnowing. The fan serves to free the good grain from its husks and this is why it has been considered as the sign of the separation of good from evil, of choice and purification. At Athens, young girls carried mystic fans in the procession at the already mentioned feast of the Thesmophoria in honor of Demeter, the goddess of wheat. In the initiation to the Lesser Mysteries at Eleusis, the initiate, his head covered with a cloth, was seated on a chair and fanned with a fan, which corresponds to a purification by air. Servius explains this rite as follows: 'Men are purified by the mysteries as wheat is purified by the fan.'[11] Christ the Winnower appears in an imposing Gospel scene that parallels that of the Apocalypse, and like it is of eschatological import:

> He that shall come after me,' says St John the Baptist, 'is mightier than I . . . whose fan is in his hand, and he will thoroughly cleanse his floor and gather his wheat into the barn; but the chaff he will burn with unquenchable fire' (Matt. 3:11–12. Cf. Isaiah 21:10).

If the phases of agricultural work represent the phases of the history of the Kingdom in general, of its historical development in the world, then the more hidden symbolism of the seed and its germination expresses rather the progress of the Kingdom in the interior of the individual, his spiritual development and his second birth and growth as 'son of God'.

> Except a corn of wheat fall into the ground and die, it abideth alone: but if it die, it bringeth forth much fruit. He that loveth his life shall lose it; and he that hateth his life in this world shall keep it unto life eternal (John 12:24–25).

The 'death' of the soul and its spiritual rebirth are magnificently symbolized by the wheat, which is scattered and buried in order to be reborn. The work of agriculture, then, depicts the work that man must accomplish in order to acquire spiritual knowledge, for this

---

11. Servius, *On the Georgics*, I, 166.

knowledge, the Word of God, is food for the soul as wheat is for the body.

This was already the meaning of the entire agricultural ritual incorporated in the Mysteries of Eleusis and its myths. In particular, this ritual involved a sacred ploughing,[12] the winnowing already mentioned, and, at the end of initiation to the Greater Mysteries, the Showing of the Ear: 'in silence', the hierophant showed the candidate a 'harvested ear of wheat'. Hippolytus of Rome, who reports this ceremony, tells us that this was the sign of spiritual regeneration. The ear of wheat is the light, sown in man at birth, which produces its fruit thanks to initiation.[13] 'The soul,' says Proclus,

> finding itself sown, that is to say, in that state that leads to birth, after the manner of a seed, must reject the species of straw and shell that come with birth, and, purifying itself of all that surrounds it, become spiritual flower and fruit. . . .[14]

Spiritual rebirth should one day have as its consequence the resurrection of the flesh, the re-conquest of a glorious body, a body of light. This is how St Paul expresses himself on the subject:

> That which thou sowest is not quickened, except it die: and that which thou sowest, thou sowest not that body that shall be, but bare grain, it may chance of wheat, or of some other grain: but God giveth it a body as it hath pleased him, and to every seed his own body. . . . Sown in corruption; it is raised in incorruption . . . sown in dishonor; it is raised in glory . . . sown in weakness; it is raised in power . . . sown a natural body; it is raised a spiritual body (1 Cor. 15:36–38 and 42–44).

Since the Christian is another Christ, it is not surprising that on occasion the grain and the ear have also symbolized Christ himself. God is then no longer the Sower and Harvester who scatters the seed and collects the grain; He has Himself become the seed and ear,

---

12. Plutarch, *Praecept. conjug.*, 42. Cf. Roscher, *Lexikon*, s.v. *Buzyges.*
13. *Philosophumena*, 5, 8 (PG 16, 3149).
14. Proclus, *In Tim.* 330A–B.

and the gift He offers is Himself as food. The Messiah is called the 'Seed of the Eternal' and 'Fruit of the earth' (Isaiah 4:2); He becomes the divine Ear in the womb of Mary assimilated to the Earth: 'Hail, untilled field that has produced the divine Ear recognized by the entire world.'[15]

In the Maronite Mass, Christ says of Himself:

I am the Bread of Life come down to earth from Heaven. . . . As a delicious grain of wheat in a fertile soil, the womb of Mary has received Me. . . .

These texts lead us to the threshold of the Eucharistic Mystery. Bread! Such is the outcome of all the work to which the wheat has been subjected: wheat become nourishment for the body, Word become food for the soul. The symbolism of the Eucharistic Bread is the blossoming of agricultural symbolism, the splendid gift of God the Farmer.

---

15. Byzantine litanies of the Most Holy Virgin. —At Eleusis, the candidate had to 'recognize' the ear that was shown him; this ear was called *Phoster*, that is to say the 'Illuminator' (*Philosophumena, loc. cit.*). And is Christ not the true *Phoster* of the world? —According to Orphism, the mystic who penetrated into the Beyond pronounced these words: 'I am the child of heaven and earth' (O. Kern, *Orph. gr. frag.* (1932), no. 32); now the ear is equally the 'child' of heaven and earth; it symbolizes their union, the principle of life. On the fact that children could be referred to as 'ears', see M.P. Milson, *Die eleusis. Gottheiten*, in *Arch. f. Religionsw.*, 1933, p18.

12

The Master
of the Vineyard

JUST AS the Eucharistic Bread is the gift of God the Farmer, so the Wine of the Sacrifice is the gift of God the Vine-grower. The symbolic developments arising from these two divine occupations correspond almost word for word with each other.

In the Old Testament the vineyard denotes the faithful people for whom the Eternal is the Vine-dresser. Psalm 80 is a wonderful elegy on the devastated vineyard, that is, Israel:

Thou hast brought a vine out of Egypt; thou hast cast out the heathen, and planted it . . . it filled the land. The hills were covered with the shadow of it, and the boughs thereof were like the goodly cedars. She sent out her boughs unto the sea, and her branches unto the rivers. . . . (the account of its devastation follows).

Elsewhere, the Lord complains that the fruit in His vineyard has not kept the promise of the blossoms.

My well-beloved hath a vineyard in a very fruitful hill: and he fenced it, and gathered out the stones thereof, and planted it with the choicest vine, and built a tower in the midst of it, and also made a winepress therein: and he looked that it should bring forth grapes, and it brought forth wild grapes.

He complains. What should he do?

I will lay it waste, [he says], there shall come up briars and thorns. . . . For the vineyard of the Lord of hosts is the house of Israel. . . . (Isaiah 5:1–7, 27:2ff.).

In the New Testament, the vineyard is the new People of God and the Kingdom of Heaven. Jesus says that 'the kingdom of heaven is like unto a man that is an householder, which went out early in the morning [and at the third, sixth, ninth and eleventh hours] to hire laborers into his vineyard' (Matt. 20:1–16). He also told another parable, which recalls the passage from Isaiah:

> There was a certain householder, which planted a vineyard, and hedged it round about, and digged a wine press in it, and built a tower and let it out to husbandmen, and went into a far country. When harvest time came, he sent his servants to collect the produce of his vineyard, but these were maltreated. Other servants suffered the same fate; finally the son of the family was himself killed; whereupon the master destroyed the scoundrels, and let out his vineyard to others. Thus the Kingdom of God will be taken away from Israel and given to other peoples. (Matt. 21:33–45).

The final phase in the work of the vineyard is the wine-harvest, which, along with the wheat-harvest in the allegories of Scripture, is the Judgment. The scene of the juridical grape-harvest is again prefigured in Isaiah in a triumphal ode:

> Who is this that cometh from Edom, with dyed garments from Bozrah? ... Wherefore art thou red in thine apparel, and thy garments like him that treadeth in the wine vat? I have trodden the winepress alone; and of the Gentiles there was none with me: for I will tread them in mine anger, and trample them in my fury; and their blood shall be sprinkled upon my garments, and I will stain all my raiment.... And I will tread down the people in mine anger, and make them drunk in my fury.... (Isaiah 6:1–6).

'He who comes from Edom,' is Christ. It is He 'that treadeth the winepress of the fierceness and wrath of Almighty God,' says the Apocalypse (19:15), which immediately after the spectacle of Christ the Reaper (14:14ff.), offers us that of Christ the Grape-gatherer and Judge. An angel carrying a sickle comes forth from the sanctuary and receives this order:

Thrust in thy sharp sickle, and gather the clusters of the vine of the earth; for her grapes are fully ripe. And the angel thrust in his sickle into the earth, and gathered the vine of the earth, and cast it into the great winepress of the wrath of God. And the winepress was trodden without the city, and blood came out of the winepress, even unto the horses' bridles.... (Apoc. 14:17–20).

Thus, in all these texts the vineyard represents the People of God, and in a more general way, humanity; the process of viniculture, directed by the heavenly Vine-grower, symbolizes history up to the Day of Judgment. This is the first aspect of the symbolism. There is a second, and more profound symbolism in which vine and wine symbolize the labor of the spiritual regeneration of humanity, which is the work of the Master of the Vineyard.

Before all else, the Vine designates the integration of the Pleroma, of the Mystical Body, composed of Christ-the-Vine-stock planted by the Father, and the man-branches, in which flows the life that wells up from the Stock.

I am the true vine, and my Father is the husbandman. Every branch in me that beareth not fruit he taketh away: and every branch that beareth fruit, he purgeth it, that it may bring forth more fruit.... I am the vine, ye are the branches.... If a man abide not in me, he is cast forth as a branch, and is withered; and men gather them, and cast them into the fire, and they are burned (John 15:1–6).

This Gospel text is glossed in a beautiful prayer said during the vigil of Pentecost before the blessing of the baptismal fonts.

God Omnipotent and Eternal, through your only Son, you have made known to your Church that you are the [heavenly] Vine-grower. With love, so that they may produce more abundant fruit, you tend the branches, which, through their union with this same Christ, the true vine, have been made fruitful. With love, you take pains that the thorn-bushes of sin do not invade the hearts of your faithful, whom you have caused to pass through the baptismal fountain, like a vine transplanted from Egypt.

Given that the Cross is, as we know, the Tree of Life, it is not surprising that, together with the Crucified One, it has been assimilated to the vine. This has been the source of abundant lyrical exposition in the liturgy:

The entire universe is covered with the laden branches of His vine; the boughs, supported by the wood of the Cross, rise up to the Kingdom of Heaven.[1]

Full of awe, the Hierarchies of bodiless Powers are there, in the presence of the Life-giving Wood. . . . Gather the living fruits offered you by Jesus, the fruitful Vine spread out upon this divine Wood.[2]

O Savior, O Christ! Like a vine attached to the Wood, You have watered the whole earth with the wine of immortality. . . . For the world, fasting is an ever pure river of immortality that flows, like another paradise, into Your life-giving Blood united with Water.[3]

Thus that magnificent image appeared in the West from which arose the symbolism of the mystical winepress, so widespread in iconography from the beginning of the fifteenth century. On the central panel of Jean Bellegambe's triptych, 'The Mystical Bath' (museum of Lille), the Cross is seen planted in the center of a vat; blood gushes from the side of Christ and flows into this vat where naked men bathe.[4] At times, the symbolism is even more forceful; the vertical branch of the cross becomes the screw of a wine-press. An old sequence of Adam of St Victor conveys the outrageous beauty of this theme of the bath of blood:

---

1. Ambrosian preface for the consecration of a cathedral (Paredi, *I Prefazi ambrosiani*, p 201).
2. Triodion of the Wednesday of the fourth week of Lent, in AL, *T. de la Passion*, p 177.
3. Triodion of the Friday of the first week of Lent, ibid., p 217.
4. E. Male, *Religious Art in France, The Late Middle Ages*, (Princeton, NJ: Princeton University Press, 1986), p 111.

Under the sacred wine-press of the Cross, the grape cluster pours itself out into the womb of the well-beloved Church; the wine flows, expressed by force, and its sweetness plunges the first-fruits of the Gentile nations into a joyous intoxication.[5]

This theme of the mystical wine-press is easily explained if we consider, as did the ancients, that in the press the living grape cluster is crushed and undergoes a 'passion', as it were, like the wheat that 'dies' in the earth. In the Dionysian Mysteries, the grape-harvest was regarded as a 'passion' of the god: Dionysius the grape, broken and trampled upon, was reborn in a drink which promised eternal happiness, for the trodden and crushed grape cluster recalled the body of the god dismembered in the vat of the Titans. Here again, as in so many other instances, the Christian tradition has quite naturally inherited these symbols which are perfectly adapted to fresh truths, so much so that, harmonizing with the Scriptural texts, they formed within the old polytheism, stones awaiting the City of God.[6]

The passion and death of the grapes is the prelude to a 'resurrection'; in disappearing, the grape cluster gives us wine. Christ the mystical grape cluster, crushed by the heavenly Vine-grower in the Passion, gives us His Blood, and the Wine He offers us, the substitute for His Blood, is truly the drink of immortality.

There are profound reasons for making wine the symbol of regeneration and eternal life, for it is the product of a natural alchemy in which vegetable water is transmuted by means of the incorporation of solar fire, the sign of the spirit. In this regard, the miracle at Cana is rich in meaning; the water in the jars denotes the nature that is transmuted into wine, or supernatural substance, under the influence of the fire of Grace. This is the spiritual alchemy that is, moreover, related to the two baptisms of water and fire. The

5. In AL, *T. pascal*, ii, p88.
6. Arnobius, *Adv. Gent.*, 5, 43; Diodorus of Sicily, 3, 62. The basic work on the correspondences between Christianity and the Dionysian Mysteries is R. Eisler, *Orphisch-Dionysische Mysteriengedanken in der christlichen Antike*,1925. Cf. REG. 1926, p67. See also A. Boulanger, *Orphée* (1925) and M.J. Lagrange, *Critique historique du Nouveau Testament, Les Mystères: l'Orphisme* (1937).

mixing of water with wine in the Mass, at the moment of the Offertory, recalls this mystery, as the prayer accompanying the rite attests:

> O God, who through a miracle created the dignity of human nature and, through an even greater miracle, reformed it, grant that through the mystery of this water and this wine we may take part in the divinity of Him who deigned to be united to our humanity, Jesus Christ.

As Adam of St Victor says above, the celestial wine gives birth within the soul to a mystical inebriation. To explain the use of wine in the Mysteries, Pausanius, one of the ancients, had already observed: 'Wine lifts men and lightens their spirit, producing the same effect as do wings with a bird.'[7] Speaking of the Apostles waiting in the Upper Room for the coming of the Spirit (Act:13), St Augustine wrote:

> They were the new wineskins; the new wine was expected from heaven, and it came, for the mysterious Cluster of Grapes was now pressed and glorified. In fact, we read in the Gospel that 'the Spirit was not yet come, for Jesus had not yet been glorified' (John 7:39).[8]

On the day of Pentecost, according to St Bernard, the Apostles were drunk with celestial wine:

> This wine was that which the true Vine had caused to flow from On-High, a wine that rejoiced the heart. . . . This wine was once found in extreme abundance in a storeroom in a spiritual place; it flooded the streets and squares of that celestial city.[9]

An eastern author shows us the martyrs, too, taken with this inebriation:

---

7. Pausanias, III, 19,6.
8. St Augustine, *Serm.* 267.
9. St Bernard, *Third Sermon for Pentecost* (PL 183, 330).

O blessed martyrs, human clusters from the Vine of God, your wine inebriates the Church. . . . When the saints come to dispose themselves at the banquet of suffering, they will drink the drink pressed by the Jews at Golgotha and so penetrate the Mysteries of God's House.[10]

St Bernard clearly defines these 'mysteries of God's House' when, in another passage, he explains the mystical inebriation as the abandonment of individual consciousness, the loss of the soul in God.[11] This, then, is the ultimate phase of the spiritual Great Work that constitutes the Sacrifice of the Mass, the offering of Bread and Wine, the first-fruits of transubstantiated nature prepared and offered by the Heavenly Farmer and Wine-grower as guarantees of our own transmutation.

---

10. Rabulas of Edessa in Bickell, *Ausg. Schrift. d. syr. Kirchenvater*, pp 262–263.
11. *On Loving God*, xi, 32 (PL 182, 9B).

Conclusion

The Spirituality of Work
and the Body Social

WE HAVE come now to the end of our enquiry, which is certainly not to say that all has been said that could be said; there are other social functions and other occupations that could also be envisaged *in divinis*. But, to begin with, the subject is new, never before, to the best of our knowledge, having been treated in a systematic fashion and as a whole. We are therefore not in a position to profit from the findings of those who, in going before us, would have opened up the way. Next, we have only included in our examination the occupations of which the symbolism is justified by explicit references to Scripture, which for us is an elementary concern of intellectual prudence when treating a subject belonging, albeit indirectly, to the doctrinal domain. Finally, we think that the examples dealt with are sufficient for our purpose, which was solely to expound the initial foundations for a spirituality of work.

To conclude, what remains is to examine the consequences flowing from the principles we have examined, as they bear upon the domains of individual and social life.

The fundamental guiding principle in our reflections implies that our daily work is a continuation of creation and consequently has its archetype in God, in Divine Activity. It is therefore legitimate to relate the different skills to God, and this is even a veritable necessity, and the only way of correctly conceiving and practicing them.

In fact, our professional activity, which occupies the greater part of our time, is thereby envisaged *sub specie aeternitas*, which in turn allows us to share in the spiritualization of skills and occupations, that is, the active life, by integrating them into the contemplative life, which is the vision of God. In his occupation, when correctly understood, man seeks to express God by means of his work, while at the same time being well aware that the occupation is not an end in itself. He knows that in his occupation, he approaches an image of God, but also that God is not fixed in this image or role. At the end of the inward journey, God 'shatters the occupations', as He shatters every symbol, finally, to reveal the Ineffable. Referring skills to divine archetypes allows all those who practice them not only to 'offer' their work to God, which goes without saying, but to 'sacralize' it to its very core, thanks to the symbol which endows it with the spiritual influence issuing from its archetype. In these conditions, there is no longer any possibility of divorce between an action that is accomplished, which, in itself, appears more or less neutral from a spiritual point of view, and the spiritual intention with which it is performed. Symbolism already integrates action spiritually, but that is not all; it essentially serves to maintain the right attitude of soul and spirit during the course of the work. In fact, it is not only the actions and tools of a trade that need to be sacralized, but action itself, man's entire active life at its source. Indeed, it is said that 'one should pray without ceasing,' prayer in all its forms being an expression of the contemplative life, itself the very goal of human life. Consequently, action, which entirely fills human life, should also become contemplative after a certain fashion.

All normal civilizations have thought and said as much in one way or another. The clearest and most detailed expression of this teaching is that transmitted to us from India in the narrative of the *Bhagavad-Gita*. The latter untiringly reminds us, from beginning to end, that God is the sole Agent, that all our acts should be referred to Him and that, consequently, our attitude should be one of *detachment*. It is upon this teaching that the spirituality of *Karma Yoga*, the Yoga of Action, is founded. We need to be *detached* from the goals and results of our actions; we should not act with the goal in mind and in view of our interest or our pleasure: above all we should act to accomplish all that doing the will of God requires. Obviously it is not a question of despising the pleasure or interest engendered by an act, but only of according them second place.

This basic doctrine, which underlies the spiritual method of *Karma Yoga* is, of course, also that of Christian spirituality, as of every method authentically having in view the 'sacralization of work', the sanctification of our actions and therefore, in the final count, of our life. This, in Christianity, is called the spirituality of the 'active life', as opposed to the spirituality of the 'contemplative life', traditionally symbolized by Martha and Mary, the two sisters of Lazarus.

Marco Pallis has correctly defined the conception of the active life in his small book mentioned in our preface. There he writes that, 'for the act to be effective it must be performed not for its own sake, but in the name of the All-giver and in imitation, on the relative plane, of the archetype of All-giving on the universal plane.'[1] If in fact action as such distracts from the essential, which is contemplation, it is necessary to find a means of transforming it in some measure into contemplation, which is life in the continual presence of God. In sum, it is a question of *sanctifying*, or better, *sacralizing* action. Now this sacralization can only be effectively realized through a gesture or a word, which integrates the action, itself initially of the purely human order, into the divine order. This gesture, which is nearly always accompanied with a word, is called a *rite*.

What needs to be thoroughly understood, however, is that this is not just any gesture or word. At issue here is a gesture or word of non-human origin, one that is transmitted by a sacred tradition, and which, by that very fact, vehicles a 'spiritual influence' and establishes contact with the divine world. Most of the time, the rite consists in saying one is going to act 'in the Name of God'. 'And whatsoever ye do in word or deed,' says St Paul, 'do all in the name of the Lord Jesus, giving thanks to God and the Father by him' (Col. 3:17). In the same way, the Muslim is invited, before commencing any activity whatsoever, to pronounce a similar formula: *Bismillah*, 'In the Name of God'.

This formula, 'in the Name of God', is full of meaning. It implies, in fact, that we recognize God as the sole source of both the energy enabling us to do what we are doing and the gift that we receive. In doing so, we become, as St Paul further says, 'laborers together with

1. *The Way and the Mountain*, p 47.

God' (1 Cor 3:9 and 10:31). In the same sense, the ancient Greeks used to say *syn theo prattein*, 'to work with God'; an expression used by Proclus in the fourth century CE as an invitation at the beginning of his commentaries on Plato's *Dialogues*, but also, eight centuries earlier, and in a very different context, by Xenophon in his *Economics*, a treatise on domestic management.

A very good example of the ritual formula 'In the Name of God' sacralizing an action can be found in the saying of grace at the beginning of a meal. By doing so, one reinstates the very material, but necessary, act of eating within the great reality of universal life, that work of the Holy Spirit at the level of the visible world. This small domestic liturgy is incorporated into the great Liturgy. In fact, the Divine Activity, through the Liturgy, the Eucharistic Liturgy above all, integrates all human activity, harmonizing it with that of God. What is more, this Eucharistic Liturgy, in its cosmic aspect, realizes the redemptive integration of the cosmos and, in principle, re-establishes order in nature, which, according to St Paul, 'is actually groaning.' For the Christian, the Great Liturgy should become the model and sanctifying instrument of his whole active life. In that regard, a prayer from the Roman Missal can be of use, for it says everything: 'Let Thy Grace, Lord, inspire our actions and support them to the end, that all our works may find their source and fulfilment in Thee.' In its conciseness, this vigorous text, which one is tempted to describe as struck after the fashion of a medal, perfectly expresses the whole of the spirituality of the active life. It unfolds, in fact, according to the movement of the divine cycle: that which comes to man from God returns to Him, at the same time leading the human subject back with itself. And this is all the more remarkable, in that we are dealing here with a 'Post Communion', that is, a prayer recited at the end of the Divine Liturgy asking God for grace to respond to what is precisely one of the fruits of this liturgy, or the Mass. Because the Mass is for the Christian the means of sanctifying his whole life, *including his active life*.

Moreover, the idea of the divine origin of the act, thus conceived, should be kept in mind throughout its accomplishment, such that it aims at the goal, which is God, instead of returning to itself, and so avoids the human subject's returning to his ego. Such is the function of the symbol. It is the tool linking the material to the spiritual, and in a way constitutes the bridge permitting circulation between them. The symbol perpetuates and radiates the "blessing" of the rite for the whole duration of the act.

When faithful to its mission, the craft guild in a traditional society ensures this sanctification of work for its members, through its particular conception, symbols, and rites, joined to the central rite of the Christian tradition.

And this leads us to recall briefly how such a society was actually organized. This conception, however, is an idea so utterly strange to the modern mentality, that what we are going to say will surprise and astonish some. This is why we wish to dwell a little more upon it and show, at least in outline, in what a traditional social community based on this symbolism consists.

To do so, we shall start by recapitulating the 'occupations of God' we have studied. We saw Him successively as scribe, physician, warrior, potter, weaver, architect, carpenter, shepherd, mariner, fisherman, hunter, gardener, farmer and wine-grower. We have deliberately arranged these occupations in their logical or rather hierarchical order. In fact, the occupations of scribe and physician are, as we said, attached to the priestly function, as the bearing of arms is to the royal, whereas all the others belong to the functions reserved to the people properly so-called: the merchants, artisans, and peasants.

What emerges is a grouping in accordance with the three 'castes' that constitute the natural social hierarchy: the Priesthood, the Monarchy, and the People. In effect, the Priesthood encompasses everything relating to the teaching of doctrine and of the sciences, subject in their entirety to Revealed Doctrine, and to worship. The Monarchy, which derives its legitimacy from the Priesthood while remaining autonomous in its sphere, is the legislative, administrative, judicial, and military function. The People, with all their intermediate bodies, also hierarchically ordered, have as their function the more or less material work necessary to the life of society.

The word 'caste' will perhaps offend certain readers, for it currently has a bad reputation. Let us explain its use. We are not here to defend the caste system, such as it might exist in this or that country and in sometimes very complicated circumstances, and which can in certain cases be criticized. But, on the other hand, we are keen to affirm that, in principle, the system of castes or of hierarchical 'orders', which does not necessarily mean that they are closed, is not only legitimate, but is even the only legitimate one. This is obvious if we take the trouble to remember that caste, in itself, denotes nothing but social function, determined on the one hand by the natural needs of the community, and on the other by the particular nature of the individual 'called' to this or that occupation. The castes, in a very general sense, are therefore integral parts of a natural society. And this is so much so that when, by some constitutional artifice, they are suppressed, it is not long before they reappear in another form. Compared to the first, the new form is in general much degraded, for the old hierarchy, based on the relative values of functions and services, now finds itself replaced by the most monstrous pseudo-hierarchy founded on money, or in a more general way, on 'economics'.

But let us return to the traditional system of castes. On the social plane, it is the reflection of the different divine activities *ad extra*, therefore a reflection of the Logos considered as the *First Born*, that is to say Archetype, *of Creation*.

This is expressed very well in figurative form by the Hindu myth of the origin of castes.[2] We learn that when Brahma created man he created him fourfold: there were originally four men. First, there was Brahman, who emerged from the mouth of Brahma and was given the Vedas, or Scriptures, so that he could teach and perform the rites. Next, Kshatriya issued from the right hand of God; his role was to defend his brother so that the latter could peacefully apply himself to devotion. Third, was Vaishya, who came forth from the right thigh to work and so feed his two elder brothers. Finally, Shudra appeared from the right foot; his job was to serve the first three. In the other versions of the myth, these four men are the sons of Purusha, who, in the Hindu tradition, corresponds to

---

2. The myth appears in different forms in the *Purusha-sukta* of the *Rig-Veda* (x, 90), the *Vishnu-Purana* (1, 6), and above all the *Laws of Manu* (*Manava-dharma-shastra*, 1, 31).

Universal Man or the Creator-Logos; this second version is in fact more exact.

The first caste, that of the 'clergy and scholars', represents contemplation, knowledge, and spiritual authority. The second embraces action in its highest form, that is, the government of men, which is temporal power. The third is devoted to the more material activity of the exploitation of the world, that is, economic, artisanal, and agricultural activity; finally, to the last caste are reserved the least noble activities, the servile and purely material and mechanical tasks. The purpose of the symbolic localization of these four castes in the four tiers of the body of Brahma—mouth, hand, thigh, and foot—is to help reveal the hierarchy. However, the fact that these four castes all issue from one and the same divine body teaches that they are all to some degree reflections of divine activities.

If, for the purposes of explanation, we have used the Hindu system, this is certainly not out of a taste for the exotic, which has nothing to do with this sort of question. It is simply because this system, its principles perfectly modeled on the natural order, helps with both the general understanding of the caste system in itself and its justification. In particular, it enables us to shed light on the social organization of Christianity, which, in the Middle Ages and particularly up to the revolution of 1789, was comparable to it.

This organization comprised three 'orders': the Clergy and Scholars, the Nobility and Knights, and the People, the latter including the fourth Hindu caste, the *shudras*, which changes nothing essential in the system.[3] By conforming to the universal and immemorial tradition, this organization permitted, within the bounds of earthly possibility, the realization of a normal social and political order.

In order to grasp the profound meaning and nature of this, let us compare the scheme of the Hindu castes with that of the social functions in their hierarchic order. We have seen that occupations are divided according to the three fundamental castes, the Priesthood, the Monarchy, and the People. Since, in a certain way, these occupations have their archetype in God himself, this amounts to

3. After a certain fashion, but only after a certain fashion, it was the *serfs* who corresponded to the *shudras*.

saying that the different social functions reflecting the divine functions, have, in a way, 'emerged' from God, like the four original men—the 'fathers of the castes'—from the body of Brahma. In Christian terms, this means that we can consider all these functions as contained 'eminently' in God, and that the *body social* is a reflection of the *Body of Christ*.

And this indeed was the way it was understood in Christianity. This social order was founded on the dogma of the Mystical Body, which corresponds *mutatis mutandis* to the teaching that sees the castes as emerging from the body of Brahma. Thus, society was conceived to be a *body*, in the full sense of the word, a fact that is often lost to sight; a multiple body, analogous to its model, the Mystical Body, Archetype of Creation, Universal Man, or again, the Pleroma. Symbolically, the Priesthood, or the hierarchic Church, corresponds to the head of Christ; the Monarchy and Knights to His arms; and the People and economic functions to His abdomen and lower limbs.

The quasi-sacramental image of this social order appeared in the seating arrangements of the faithful inside the basilica or cathedral, itself an architectural image of the Pleroma. At great feasts, the Bishop, representing the spiritual authority, sat in the choir (the head), the King and Nobles at the entrance to the choir and filling the transept (the arms), and the People in the nave, with the master artisans—the social authorities—at their head.[4]

Thus an organic order existed, an organism at once temporal and spiritual, a prolongation or reflection on the social plane of the Heavenly Jerusalem, which is the fulfillment of the Pleroma.[5] It was a normally living and breathing organism: the impulse from the spiritual caste descended and circulated through, and thanks to, the subordinate orders, which, like 'relays', placed the sacred truths and values from the head within the reach of everyone, these truths alone having the ability to order all contingent activities to eternal salvation, the essential goal and final end of temporal society.

4. L. Lallemant, *La Vocation de l'Occident* (1947), p 200.
5. Significant, in this regard, is the designation of the king as 'Lieutenant of God' and 'Vicar Temporal of Christ'.

Clearly, it is at the level of these 'relays' that the symbolism of the occupations played its role, symbolism that, in some measure, conveyed spiritual grace on the plane of action.

Such is the model of every society worthy of the name. In its hierarchy founded on the natural order, an order ready to receive supernatural illumination, it knows nothing, to be sure, of egalitarian and libertarian myths. Nevertheless, it guarantees to the extent humanly possible, not only true equity, which consists in each finding within his own order the means of self-realization, but true freedom, which consists in determining the means of attaining the spiritual end of man in his passage through this world. Social subversion is born, precisely, in the overturning of this authentic hierarchy and its replacement with a false one of a materialist nature.

Any restoration of society and work which does not start from these principles—intangible as they are, and whatever their adaptation to the present conditions of the world, certainly different from those of days gone by—is bound to fail. We hope some day to show this in a more specialized study. In fact, the present book which, as we said at the beginning, is only intended to be a collection of preliminary reflections, logically demands two lines of development, one bearing upon the spirituality of the active life and the other upon the restoration of a sacred sociology and politics. God willing, they shall be undertaken.

'

Abbreviations

AL: Dom P. Gueranger, *L'Année Liturgique.*

CRAI; *Comptes rendus de l'Academie des Inscriptions et Belles-Lettres,* Paris.

DAC: Dom Leclercq, *Dictionnaire d'Archéologie chrétienne.*

DAGR: Dahremberg, Saglio et Pottier, *Dictionnaire des Antiquités grecques et romaines.*

ET: *Etudes Traditionnelles,* Paris.

MD: La *Maison-Dieu,* Paris.

OS: *L'Orient Syrien,* Vernon.

PG: *Patrologiae Graeca* (Migne).

PL: *Patrologiae Latina* (Migne).

PO: *Patrologie orientale* (Graffin-Nau).

RA: *Revue Africaine,* Paris.

RCAP: *Rendiconti dell'Academia Pontificia,* Rome.

REG: *Revue des Etudes grecques,* Paris.